CAN·AM Cooks

Comfort Food
from Around the World

by
Willie Fitzpatrick
Food Writer for the Calgary Sun

Front Cover
Oriental Chicken Stir-Fry, page 141
Hot Thai Vegetable Salad, page 69

CAN•AM Cooks
by
Willie Fitzpatrick

Revised Edition – January 1998

Published by
Centax Books & Distribution
1150 Eighth Avenue
Regina, Saskatchewan
Canada S4R 1C9

Canadian Cataloguing in Publication Data

Fitzpatrick, Wilhemina, 1958 -

Can•Am Cooks

Includes index.
ISBN 1-895292-99-9

1. Cookery, International.   I. Title.

TX725.F57 1994   641.59   C94-920026-3

Photography by:
Ross C. (Hutch) Hutchinson
Hutchinson and Company
Calgary, Alberta

Dishes and Accessories Compliments of:
Benkris, Calgary, Alberta

Pottery Plates and Bowl by potters:
Mel Bolen, Humboldt, Sask. – Front Cover & page 155
Zach Dietrich, Moose Jaw, Sask. – page 51

Designed, Printed and Produced in Canada by:
Centax Books, a Division of PrintWest Communications Ltd.
Publishing Director, Photo Designer & Food Stylist: Margo Embury
1150 Eighth Avenue, Regina, Saskatchewan, Canada S4R 1C9
(306) 525-2304 FAX: (306) 757-2439

TABLE OF CONTENTS

Recipes have been tested in U.S. Standard measurements. Common metric measurements are given as a convenience for those who are more familiar with metric. Recipes have not been tested in metric.

Fundraising Partnership

Can-Am Police-Fire Games and PrintWest are pleased to be able to jointly develop this cookbook as a fundraising opportunity for the many worthwhile community, charitable, athletic and youth projects sponsored by Police and Fire Services across North America.

If your organization is interested in a similar project
FAX Toll-Free to: PrintWest Communications Ltd.
                            1-800-823-682

3

THE CAN-AM CONCEPT

The mission of the Can-Am Police-Fire Games is to promote camaraderie and physical fitness among and between law enforcement and fire service agencies and personnel through Olympic-style sports and events. The Can-Am logo depicts the unification between the United States and Canada to meet a common goal.

The Can-Am Police-Fire Games embody good will and an international spirit of participation and competition. Police and Firefighters from any country are eligible to compete in a dynamic week-long festival promoting physical excellence and unique skills.

Gold, silver, and bronze medals are awarded in 47 individual and team events. Competitions include wide-ranging individual athletic performances (track and field, biathlon, triathlon, decathlon, golf, karate, cycling, waterskiing, and toughest competitor alive), team events (hockey, basketball, volleyball, softball, and paintball), shooting sports (rifle, trapshooting, skeet, pistol, and archery), and professional events (S.W.A.T., canine, toughest firefighter alive, and motorcycle rodeo), just to name a few in each category.

Up to 3000 police and firefighters participate in the Can-Am Police-Fire Games. The games incorporate several vital objectives involving positive public awareness of police and firefighters' services, raising funds for charities such as Burn Units and Special Olympics, developing camaraderie between police and fire agencies, encouraging professional and personal development, and challenging both law enforcement and fire services to create programs that promote physical fitness throughout their agencies.

Your purchases of *CAN•AM Cooks* will help support individual and team participation in the Can-Am Police-Fire Games, and help raise funds for police and firefighters' public charities. We hope that you enjoy this international collection of fabulous make-ahead recipes for busy cooks. **Thank you for your support.**

ACKNOWLEDGEMENT

CAN-AM Games gratefully acknowledge **FUJIFILM** for their support of the first edition of *Can•Am Cooks* as a fundraiser for the many worthwhile community, charitable and athletic projects for Police and Fire Services across North America.

APPETIZERS & DRINKS

SHRIMP-STUFFED TOMATOES

A make-ahead dish.
Serves 6 as a starter.

These make a beautiful and substantial opener to a nice dinner. If you can't find cilantro, try another fresh herb such as basil.

¼ cup	olive oil	60 mL
1	lime, juice of (about 1½ tbsp. [60 mL])	1
¼ cup	chopped fresh cilantro	60 mL
¼ tsp.	pepper	1 mL
½ cup	finely chopped green pepper	125 mL
¼ cup	finely chopped green onion	60 mL
36	large shrimp (about 1 lb. [500 g]), cooked	36
6	large, ripe tomatoes	6

Combine the oil, lime juice, cilantro and pepper and mix well. Add the green pepper and green onion and mix again. Add the shrimp and stir gently. Set aside.

Cut the tomatoes across 3 times (crossing in the middle as if into 6 wedges), but do not cut all the way through the bottom. Each tomato should still be in 1 piece, with the wedges slightly separated, but still joined at the bottom.

Place a shrimp between each wedge in each tomato, then spoon some dressing over the top of each tomato and down the center so it runs into the tomato. (These can be made ahead, covered and refrigerated until about 1 hour before serving. Spoon dressing back over the stuffed tomatoes.)

To Serve: Place each tomato on a few leaves of butter lettuce on a small plate.

SHRIMP-STUFFED AVOCADOS

A partial make-ahead dish.
Serves 6 as a starter.

A colorful first course to get the taste buds jumping.

¼ cup	mayonnaise, regular or low-fat	60 mL
¼ cup	sour cream, regular or low-fat	60 mL
1 tsp.	curry powder	5 mL
½	bright red apple, peel on, cored, finely chopped	½
¼ cup	finely chopped sweet red pepper	60 mL
¼ cup	finely chopped red onion	60 mL
1 tbsp.	lime juice	15 mL
4	drops Tabasco	4
4 oz.	cooked salad shrimp (not canned)	115 g
3	ripe avocados	3
2 tsp.	lemon juice	10 mL

Mix the mayonnaise, sour cream, curry powder, apple, red pepper, red onion, lime juice and Tabasco. Gently stir in the shrimp. Let sit for ½ hour. (Make this ahead to this point, cover and refrigerate until about 1 hour before serving.)

Just before serving, cut the avocados in half lengthwise and discard pits. Scrape the cavity lightly with a fork to loosen the pulp and make the cavities more rounded. Brush the surface lightly with lemon juice. Fill the cavities with the shrimp mixture and serve.

Note: Do not cut the avocados until you are ready to serve them because they brown very quickly.

FETA-STUFFED AVOCADOS

A partial make-ahead dish.
Serves 4 as a starter.

⅔ cup	small cubes feta cheese	150 mL
¼ cup	short slivers sweet red pepper	60 mL
2 tbsp.	finely chopped green onion	30 mL
¼ cup	sliced black olives	60 mL
½ tsp.	dried oregano leaves	2 mL
2 tbsp.	olive oil	30 mL
1 tbsp.	raspberry or cider vinegar	15 mL
2	ripe avocados	2
1 tsp.	lemon juice	5 mL

Combine the feta, red pepper, green onion, olives, oregano, oil and vinegar. Stir well and set aside. (This stuffing can be made ahead to this point, covered and refrigerated until about 1 hour before serving.)

Just before serving, carefully cut the avocados in half lengthwise. Remove the pit and discard. With a fork, scrape the cavity a little to loosen the pulp and make the cavity more rounded. Brush the surface of the pulp with the lemon juice. Fill the cavities with the feta mixture and serve.

Note: Do not cut the avocados until you are ready to serve them because they brown very quickly.

CHICKEN LIVER PÂTÉ

A make-ahead dish.
Makes about 2 cups (500 mL).

This is a less fatty version of a traditional pâté. It is very peppery, especially if you use 2 full tablespoons (30 mL) of peppercorns.

¼ cup	butter	60 mL
1-2 tbsp.	whole black peppercorns (according to taste)	15-30 mL
¼ cup	minced onion	60 mL
¾ lb.	chicken livers, chopped	365 g
2 tbsp.	dark rum or brandy	30 mL
½ tsp.	salt	2 mL
2 tbsp.	chicken broth	30 mL

Melt the butter over medium heat, add peppercorns and onion and cook for about 2 minutes. Add the chicken livers and continue cooking until the meat is no longer pink.

Put into a blender; add the rest of the ingredients; blend until smooth. Pour into a serving dish and refrigerate at least 4 hours. Be sure to cover the pâté if it is going to be in the refrigerator much longer than that.

To serve: Serve with mustard on the side, with thin slices of plain or rye bread, or crackers.

If you need a small amount of liqueur for a recipe, buy one of the 2 oz. (60 mL) bottles available at most liquor outlets in a wide variety of liqueurs. Perhaps even keep one each of orange liqueur, brandy, sherry and coffee liqueur on hand — they do wonders for a plain dessert or recipe.

DEVILLED EGGS WITH CAPERS
A make-ahead dish.
Makes 20 pieces.

The salty pickled flavors of capers & olives suit the devilled eggs perfectly.

10	small eggs, hard-boiled	10
¼ cup	mayonnaise (regular or low-fat)	60 mL
1 tbsp.	prepared mustard	15 mL
¼ cup	chopped pimiento-stuffed green olives	60 mL
1 tbsp.	chopped capers	15 mL

Carefully shell the eggs; cut in half lengthwise and scoop out the yolk into a bowl. Add the mayonnaise and the mustard and mix until smooth. Stir in the olives and capers. Spoon evenly into the 20 egg whites. (This can be made ahead, covered and refrigerated for a day.) Serve close to room temperature.

Note: Capers are pungent, pickled flower buds, from bushes found in the Mediterranean region. Sun dried, the buds are pickled in vinegar brine or salted. They vary considerably in size and the smallest are the most flavorful. A classic accompaniment to smoked salmon, try them in sauces and with meats and vegetables. Nasturtium buds and seeds have a peppery flavor. They can be pickled and used like capers.

BAKED SCOTCH EGGS
A make-ahead dish.
Serves 6 as a starter.

Try these as an opening course for a Robbie Burns' night, or for Christmas morning. They're really good, without the fuss or the extra fat of deep-fat frying.

13 oz.	sausage meat	375 g
1/2 tsp.	ground dried rosemary	2 mL
2 tsp.	Dijon mustard	10 mL
1/4 cup	fine fresh bread crumbs	60 mL
6	small eggs, hard-boiled, shelled	6
1 cup	fine dry bread crumbs	250 mL
2	eggs, beaten	2
2 tbsp.	sherry	30 mL

Preheat oven to 375°F (190°C).

Combine the sausage meat, rosemary, mustard and fresh bread crumbs and mix well. Divide into 6 portions. Flatten each portion in the palm of your hand. Put a hard-boiled egg in the center and mold the sausage mixture around the egg to cover *completely*. Set aside on some waxed paper.

Combine the raw eggs and sherry in a bowl and mix well. Roll each sausage-covered egg in dry crumbs, then in a mixture of egg and sherry, then in crumbs again. On an ungreased cookie sheet, bake for about 30 minutes, until nicely browned. Serve hot, warm or cold. (These can be made ahead and refrigerated. However, because of the eggs, they do not freeze well.)

To serve: Place on lettuce leaves, serve with hot mustard or sweet mustard pickles. For a luncheon, add salad. You could also cut them into wedges and serve as a finger food, or as an addition to a mixed appetizer plate.

TSATSIKI
A make-ahead dish.
Makes about 2 cups (500 mL).

There are many versions of this delightful dip — this one is quite a bit lower in fat than many others because there is no added oil.

1	8-10" (20-25 cm) long English cucumber	1
½ tsp.	salt	2 mL
½ cup	yogurt	125 mL
½ cup	sour cream	125 mL
2	garlic cloves, crushed, or more, to taste	2
1 tsp.	crumbled dried mint or 1 tbsp. (15 mL) chopped fresh mint	5 mL

Wash and trim the cucumber; shred finely with a grater, discarding any large pieces of peel. Spread shredded cucumber over bottom and sides of a colander. Sprinkle with salt. Put the colander in a bowl and leave for an hour or so, then squeeze the grated cucumber to get out as much water as possible.

Mix the grated cucumber with the rest of the ingredients. Refrigerate at least a few hours to let the flavors blend. (This can be made ahead, covered and refrigerated for several days.) Bring close to room temperature before serving with pita bread or crisp, raw vegetables.

Variations: For a change of texture and flavor, add ¼ cup (60 mL) very finely minced red onion.

For a low-fat version use skim-milk yogurt and non-fat sour cream.

*Use skim-milk yogurt cheese to replace yogurt and sour cream. To make **Skim-Milk Yogurt Cheese**, place 2 cups (500 mL) of natural skim-milk yogurt (no gelatin) in a cheesecloth-lined sieve over a bowl. Cover and refrigerate for about 24 hours. This will yield about 1 cup (250 mL) of yogurt cheese.*

HOMMOUS

A make-ahead dish.
Makes about 2 cups (500 mL).

Also spelled Hummus, Hoummus or Houmos, this popular and nutritious Middle Eastern dip can become addictive. The addition of the pickled jalapeño juice gives this a tiny zing that makes all the difference. You can garnish the top with one or two slices of jalapeño or other hot peppers.

19 oz.	can chick peas, drained, ¼ cup (60 mL) juice reserved	540 mL
¼ cup	tahini (see note)	60 mL
¼ cup	olive oil	60 mL
¼ cup	lemon juice	60 mL
1 tbsp.	pickled jalapeño pepper juice or ¼ tsp. (1 mL) Tabasco	15 mL
2	garlic cloves, crushed, or more, to taste	2

Put everything in a blender and blend until smooth. (This can be made ahead, covered and refrigerated for up to a week.)

Serve with fresh pita bread triangles or crisp raw vegetables. If you have leftovers, try using it as a spread in a sandwich.

Variation: To make a low-fat version, eliminate or decrease the olive oil and increase the chick pea juice and lemon juice to obtain the desired consistency and flavor.

Note: If you run out of tahini or can't get a jar in any of the local stores, try using peanut butter. Replacing the required amount of tahini with half the amount of peanut butter actually produces a reasonable facsimile. So, if you simply cannot find tahini, use 2 tbsp. (30 mL) peanut butter instead.

For a change in sandwich spreads, try chutney (hot or mild) instead of mayonnaise or butter. It tastes great and is usually very low in fat.

BRUSCHETTA
A make-ahead dish.
Makes about 2 cups (500 mL).

Sometimes I add up to ¼ cup (60 mL) first-pressed olive oil to this recipe, and sometimes (when I'm fat conscious) I don't add any oil at all. How's that for a recipe!

6	ripe tomatoes, finely chopped	6
¼ cup	finely chopped fresh basil (must be fresh!)	60 mL
3	garlic cloves, crushed, or more, to taste	3
½ tsp.	salt	2 mL
2-4 tbsp.	finely chopped pickled jalapeño peppers	30-60 mL
2 tbsp.	balsamic or red wine vinegar	30 mL
2-4 tbsp.	extra virgin olive oil (optional)	30-60 mL

Put the chopped tomatoes in a colander and shake for about 15 seconds to remove the excess liquid and seeds. Put the tomatoes and everything else in a glass bowl, mix well, cover and refrigerate for several hours. Serve close to room temperature. Stir again before serving. (This can be made ahead, covered and refrigerated for 2 days.)

To serve: Spread on thin slices of Italian bread, or top oven-toasted baguette slices with this flavorful mixture. For added zest, rub a cut clove of garlic over the toasted baguette slices. See also the Mexican Bruschetta, page 49, for a very different version.

Variation: Add ¼ cup (60 mL) chopped, oil-packed, sun-dried tomatoes.

Note: There are many varieties and grades of olive oil available from France, Italy, Spain and the U.S. Cold-pressed oils are the best and, of these, extra virgin, the first pressing, is the finest quality. A more green color indicates a more intense flavor. Pure or virgin olive oil is less expensive and is recommended for frying or high heat recipes. The intense flavor of extra virgin olive oil breaks down at high temperatures so the extra expense is wasted. Light olive oil is a filtered oil that has little color or flavor. It is good for cooking and baking where the olive flavor is not desirable, but the benefits of a monounsaturated fat are wanted. It also has a higher smoke point and so is good for use in frying.

See photograph on page 51.

COZUMEL SALSA
A make-ahead dish.
Makes about 2 cups (500 mL).

Wonderfully fresh and biting — this is a version of the Nepec salsa served in Cozumel.

2	firm ripe tomatoes, finely chopped	2
1/2	large white or red onion, finely chopped	1/2
2	limes, juice of (about 3 tbsp. [45 mL])	2
3 tbsp.	chopped, pickled jalapeño peppers, or to taste	45 mL
4 tsp.	pickled jalapeño pepper juice	20 mL
1/4 cup	finely chopped fresh cilantro	60 mL

Put the tomatoes in a colander and shake gently for about 15 seconds to remove excess juice and seeds. Mix everything together in a glass dish and refrigerate for several hours or longer. This can be made ahead, covered and refrigerated for several days.

To serve: Serve with tortilla chips or use in the Nachos recipes, pages 17-19 or the Mexican Bruschetta, page 49.

Recipes are almost always adaptable to personal taste. If you love spicy hot dishes, add a little extra of the "hot" spice in curry and other spicy dishes. Garlic lovers, use larger cloves or add an extra clove or two. The reverse applies too. Go easy on the spices if your stomach seems to prefer it that way.

GUACAMOLE
A make-ahead dish.
Makes about 2 cups (500 mL).

Be sure the avocados are ripe, just slightly soft to the touch. If they're too hard they simply will not taste good. The jalapeños give this a little bite.

4	ripe avocados	4
2	limes, juice of (about 3 tbsp. [45 mL])	2
2	ripe tomatoes, finely chopped	2
2	green onions, finely chopped	2
1 tbsp.	finely chopped pickled jalapeño peppers	15 mL
¼ cup	pickled jalapeño pepper juice	60 mL

Peel avocados and discard the pits. Mash the pulp well and mix immediately with lime juice.

Toss the tomatoes gently in a colander for about 10 seconds to remove excess juice and seeds. Add tomatoes to the mashed avocados along with the rest of the ingredients; stir well. Serve close to room temperature. (This can be made ahead, covered and refrigerated for several hours.) Stir well before serving because the surface may be slightly discolored.

To serve: Serve with tortilla chips or with the nachos recipes, pages 17-19.

Avocados can be very expensive at times. To stretch guacamole, add ¼ cup (60 mL) yogurt for each avocado. You may want to increase the spices to make up for the added yogurt.

Nachos — Super Simple
So, so simple.
Serves 4 as a snack.

Very easy and quick for when you've got the craving, but not the time or the energy to do a lot of chopping.

8 oz.	plain tortilla chips	250 g
6-8 oz.	cheese (mozzarella, Cheddar, colby), grated	170-250 g
2/3 cup	salsa	150 mL

Preheat oven to 350°F (180°C).

Spread the chips over 1 or 2 cookie sheets in almost a single layer — they can overlap slightly. Sprinkle the cheese over the chips, and then dot the cheese with ½ teaspoonfuls (2 mL) of salsa. Bake for 10-15 minutes, until the cheese is melted and bubbly.

Nachos — Basic
Very basic.
Serves 4-6 as a snack.

For those of you who can't be bothered with all those healthy vegetables, here's the basic recipe.

8 oz.	plain tortilla chips	250 g
6-8 oz.	cheese (mozzarella, Cheddar, colby), grated	170-250 g
¼-½ cup	chopped pickled jalapeño peppers (optional)	60-125 mL
2 cups	Cozumel salsa (page 15) or commercial salsa	500 mL
1 cup	yogurt or sour cream	250 mL

Preheat oven to 350°F (180°C).

Spread chips over 1 or 2 cookie sheets in almost a single layer — they can overlap slightly. Sprinkle the cheese over the chips, and then the jalapeños. Bake for about 10-15 minutes, until the cheese is melted and bubbly. Serve with the salsa and yogurt on the side for dipping.

Nachos — Not So Basic
Serves 6 as a snack, or serves 2-3 for supper!

This is super weekend fare — the kids in bed, a good video rented, and a big serving of nachos.

8 oz.	plain tortilla chips	250 g
6-8 oz.	cheese (mozzarella, Cheddar, colby), grated	170-250 g
1/2	green pepper, chopped	1/2
1	tomato, chopped	1
3	green onions, chopped	3
1/4-1/2 cup	sliced jalapeño peppers (pickled or fresh, seeded, optional)	60-125 mL
1/2 cup	sliced black olives	125 mL
1/2 cup	cooked, crumbled ground beef (optional)	125 mL
1 cup	Cozumel salsa (page 15) or commercial salsa	250 mL
1 cup	yogurt or sour cream	250 mL
1 cup	guacamole (page 16)	250 mL

Preheat oven to 350°F (180°C).

Spread the chips over 1 or 2 cookie sheets in an almost single layer — they can overlap slightly. Sprinkle the cheese over the chips, then sprinkle on green pepper, tomato, onions, jalapeño peppers, olives, and beef, if using. Bake for 10-15 minutes, until the cheese is melted and bubbly.

To Serve: Serve with bowls of salsa, yogurt or sour cream, and guacamole for dipping.

NACHOS GRANDE
Serves 4 as a main course.

A wonderful messy meal for the true blue nacho fan — this is great fun for the ultimate casual meal with good friends.

	ingredients for NACHOS — NOT SO BASIC (page 18) plus:	
4 cups	shredded iceberg lettuce	1 L
14 oz.	can refried beans	398 mL
2 tbsp.	water	30 mL

Preheat oven to 350°F (180°C).

Using the same ingredients as NACHOS — NOT SO BASIC, page 18, have each person put a layer of tortilla chips on individual ovenproof plates. Top the chips, according to personal taste, with cheese, green pepper, tomato, green onion, jalapeño peppers, olives, and ground beef, if using. Bake for 10-15 minutes, until the cheese is melted and bubbly.

Meanwhile, arrange lettuce, salsa, yogurt or sour cream and guacamole in bowls on the counter, buffet-style. Mix the refried beans with the water, and heat until very hot (about 3 minutes in the microwave) and add to the "buffet". When the nachos are cooked, each person removes his own plate from the oven and quickly puts it on the counter (it's hot!!). Each person tops his nachos with lettuce and sauces, according to taste. Provide good-sized napkins — this is messy! A fork helps get the final tidbits off the plate, too.

BAKED ARTICHOKES with Cilantro
A partial make-ahead dish.
Serves 4.

This very easy and flavorful munchy is a little messy. You may want to give everyone a small plate and a fork instead of using a communal dish.

2 tbsp.	olive oil	30 mL
1 tbsp.	lime juice	15 mL
2	garlic cloves, crushed	2
1/2 tsp.	dried oregano leaves	2 mL
1/4 cup	fresh cilantro leaves	60 mL
14 oz.	can artichoke hearts, drained, quartered	398 mL
2	tomatoes, coarsely chopped	2

Preheat oven to 300°F (150°C).

Mix the oil, lime juice, garlic, oregano, and cilantro. Put the artichokes and tomatoes in a 8" (20 cm) square glass casserole; pour the oil mixture over and stir to coat. (You can make this ahead to this point, cover and refrigerate, and add 5 minutes baking time.)

Bake for 15 minutes.

To Serve: Serve with sliced French bread.

If you are making a recipe that you want to make ahead and bake and serve later, add some extra baking time to compensate for the coldness of the dish from the refrigerator.

BRANDIED BRIE with Apricots
A partial make-ahead dish.
Serves 4.

Serve this as a predinner munchy, but it is also very good as a dessert with fruit.

4.5 oz.	round of Brie or Camembert cheese	125 g
2 tbsp.	brandy	30 mL
10	dried apricots, chopped	10

Preheat oven to 350°F (180°C).

Place the cheese in a small ovenproof dish, just large enough to fit the cheese with about 1" (2.5 cm) all around for the apricots.

Make slashes in the top of the Brie (not through the sides) so that some of the brandy can seep into the cheese. Pour 1 tbsp. (15 mL) of the brandy slowly over the cheese so that as much as possible goes into the slashes. Mix the other 1 tbsp. (15 mL) of brandy with the apricots, then sprinkle the apricots around the brie. Cover tightly with foil. (You can make this ahead to this point, refrigerate, and add 5 minutes baking time.)

Bake for about 20 minutes. The cheese should be runny and hot when you cut into it.

To Serve: Serve with water crackers or other plain crackers.

SIMPLE SWISS FONDUE

Serves 4 as a starter; 2 as a light meal.

This is incredibly easy and simple, with only 4 ingredients.

8 oz.	Emmenthal cheese, finely grated	250 g
1 tbsp.	cornstarch	15 mL
1/2 cup	dry white wine	125 mL
1/4 cup	dry sherry	60 mL

Mix the cheese and cornstarch together until well-combined.

Put the wine and sherry in the top of a double boiler, with boiling water in the bottom half, and heat set to maintain a rigorous boil. Heat the wine and sherry until very hot. Add about 1/5 of the cheese and stir vigorously with a wire whisk until melted. Continue this process until all the cheese has been added. At this point the sauce will be thick and ready to serve, although it will keep nicely, covered, over low heat for 30 minutes or so. Just remember to stir vigorously before serving.

To Serve: Serve with fresh cubes of French bread to dip into the sauce. Crisp, fresh vegetables could be used as dippers also. If serving as a light meal, serve with a salad and a light fruit dessert.

SPINACH & FETA PHYLLO

A make-ahead dish.
Serves 12 as a starter.

Relax — phyllo is really not that difficult to work with. Just move quickly and keep it covered. It's versatile too. These make great finger foods if cut small, or cut them larger for a sit-down appetizer. Keep out as many as you want to use now and freeze the rest. Use leftover sheets of Phyllo to make Beef And Pine Nut Phyllo, page 24, or make about half of this recipe again, doubling the sheets over to create the same number of layers.

2	eggs	2
10 oz.	pkg. frozen chopped spinach, thawed, well-drained	285 g
2 cups	grated feta cheese	500 mL
1/2 cup	minced green onion	125 mL
1/3 cup	yogurt	75 mL
2	garlic cloves, crushed, or more, to taste	2
1/4 tsp.	pepper	1 mL
1/4 tsp.	dried dill	1 mL
12-14	sheets of phyllo pastry (frozen, thawed)	12-14
1/2 cup	butter, melted	125 mL

Preheat oven to 350°F (180°C).

Beat the eggs, add spinach, feta, onion, yogurt, garlic, pepper and dill. Mix well and set aside.

Read the instructions on the phyllo package as to how to handle it. Lay 1 sheet of the phyllo on a large greased shallow pan that is as close to the size of the sheet of phyllo as possible. If there is a little excess, let it stick out over the side and fold it over just before baking. Brush phyllo all over very lightly with butter. Repeat phyllo and butter 6 or 7 times. Spread filling evenly over the top of the phyllo, and top with 6 or 7 more layers of phyllo brushed with butter.

Press the overhanging phyllo onto the edge of the main portion. Cut with a very sharp, pointed knife into the desired sizes; diamonds or squares are usual. Bake for about 25 minutes, until lightly browned. Serve hot, warm or cold. (This can be made ahead and eaten within a couple of days, or wrapped well and frozen.)

Variation: For a lower-fat version, spray every other sheet of phyllo with butter-flavored cooking spray. Use 1/2 the amount of butter and keep it hot so less will be needed to lightly brush the other phyllo sheets.

BEEF & PINE NUT PHYLLO

A make-ahead dish.
Serves 6-8 as a starter.

One package of phyllo dough is sufficient for 1 batch of this recipe and 1 of Spinach and Feta Phyllo, page 23. Again, serve as finger foods, sit-down appetizers, or even as a luncheon with a salad.

1 lb.	lean ground beef	500 g
2/3 cup	finely chopped tomato	150 mL
2	garlic cloves	2
1	onion, minced	1
1 tsp.	garam masala, or 1/2 tsp. (2 mL) each cinnamon and curry powder	5 mL
1/4 cup	pine nuts	60 mL
1/2 cup	chopped fresh parsley	125 mL
1/2 tsp.	cinnamon	2 mL
1	lemon, juice of (about 2 tbsp. [30 mL])	1
6-8	sheets phyllo pastry, halved (frozen, thawed)	6-8
1/4 cup	butter	60 mL

Preheat oven to 350°F (180°C).

Over medium-high heat, fry the ground beef, tomato, garlic, onion, garam masala, pine nuts and parsley until ground beef is fully cooked and the onion is soft. Stir frequently. Drain off the excess fat. Stir in the cinnamon and lemon juice.

Lay 1/2 sheet of phyllo on a greased shallow pan that is as close to the size of the pastry as possible. Brush very lightly with butter. Repeat with half the pastry sheets. Spread the beef filling evenly over the buttered pastry sheets, and top with remaining layers of phyllo and butter until all the pastry is used up.

Cut with a very sharp, pointed knife into the desired size. Bake for about 25 minutes, until nicely browned. Serve hot, warm or cold. (This can an be made ahead and eaten within a couple of days, or wrapped well and frozen.)

Note: Pine nuts are expensive but necessary, so refrigerate (up to 3 months) or freeze (up to 9 months) any leftover nuts. Slivered almonds may be substituted if you're desperate but the flavor is not the same.

Variation: See lower-fat variation on page 23.

HOT JAMAICAN WINGS
A partial make-ahead dish.
Marinating time is required.
Serves 6-8.

Jamaican Jerk Wings — these tropical treats are great at a party. Most of the work can be done the day before so all you have to do is bake them. They are quite hot on the tongue, and messy, so pass along lots of napkins.

3 lb.	chicken wings and/or drummettes	1.5 kg
¼ cup	orange juice concentrate	60 mL
2 tbsp.	oil	30 mL
2 tbsp.	raspberry or red wine vinegar	30 mL
2 tbsp.	sherry or white wine	30 mL
1 tbsp.	dark soy sauce	15 mL
1 tbsp.	brown sugar	15 mL
1 tsp.	salt	5 mL
1 tsp.	pepper	5 mL
1 tsp.	oregano	5 mL
1 tsp.	cinnamon	5 mL
4	1" (2.5 cm) dried red chili peppers	4
3	garlic cloves, crushed	3
½ cup	chopped green onion	125 mL

Halve the wings at the joint and put in a glass bowl.

Put everything else in a blender and blend until smooth, then pour this over the wings and stir well to coat. Cover and refrigerate 4 hours or overnight. Stir occasionally.

Preheat oven to 425°F (220°C). Place the wings in a single layer, fat side down, in a foil-lined shallow pan. (Reserve marinade.) Bake 15 minutes. Turn and brush with marinade. Bake for another 15 minutes, until completely cooked.

SMOKED SALMON SPREAD
A partial make-ahead dish.
Serves 6.

This is so easy, yet rich and impressive. Be sure to buy chunk smoked salmon rather than lox — it will be a fraction of the price.

6 oz.	cream cheese, softened (regular or low-fat)	170 g
½ cup	sour cream (regular or low-fat)	125 mL
1 tbsp.	lemon juice	15 mL
½ tsp.	dried dill	2 mL
4 oz.	smoked salmon chunk, finely chopped	115 g
1 tbsp.	fine bread crumbs	15 mL

Preheat oven to 350°F (180°C).

Cream the cheese well, add the sour cream, lemon juice, dill and smoked salmon. Mix well, put in a 3 x 5" (7 x 13 cm) ovenproof dish and sprinkle the bread crumbs on top. (You can prepare this ahead to this point, cover and refrigerate, and add 5 minutes baking time.)

Bake for 15 minutes, until very hot and bubbling slightly around the edges.

To Serve: Serve with plain crackers or small thin slices of rye bread.

SMOKED SALMON RAMEKINS

A partial make-ahead dish.
Serves 6 as a starter.

These smoky starters are like a light seafood lasagne. They make a very ample first course, or they would do nicely with a salad for a light meal. Be sure to buy chunk smoked salmon rather than lox — it will be a fraction of the price. Don't worry too much about all the little measurements — just try to keep things fairly even.

8 oz.	cream cheese, softened	250 g
2 cups	cool chicken broth	500 mL
9	oven-ready lasagne noodles	9
6 oz.	smoked salmon chunk, finely chopped	170 g
½ cup	capers, drained	125 mL
2 cups	grated mozzarella cheese	500 mL

Preheat oven to 375°F (190°C).

Using an electric mixer, beat the cheese until creamy. Slowly add broth, beating well until smooth.

Lightly grease 6, 3 x 5" (7 x 13 cm) ovenproof dishes. Crack the lasagne noodles in halves or pieces so they will fit the dishes as you need them.

Put 1 tbsp. (15 mL) sauce in the bottom of each dish, top each with ½ a lasagne noodle, ½ oz. (1 tbsp. [15 mL]) of smoked salmon, a few capers, 2 tbsp. (30 mL) of sauce, ½ a lasagne noodle, ½ oz. (1 tbsp. [15 mL]) of smoked salmon, a few capers, 2 tbsp. (30 mL) of sauce, ½ a lasagna noodle, 2 tbsp. (30 mL) of sauce and top with mozzarella. Cover each closely with foil. (You can make ahead to this point, refrigerate, and add 5-10 minutes baking time.)

Bake for 30 minutes. Remove foil. Bake another 10 minutes.

Note: You could bake this in a 9" (23 cm) square glass dish if you don't want individual dishes. Add 10 minutes baking time.

HOT CRAB DIP

**A partial make-ahead dish.
Serves 6.**

A rich and creamy dish to pamper your friends, or just yourselves.

4 oz.	cream cheese, softened (regular or low-fat)	115 g
2 tbsp.	lemon juice	30 mL
4 oz.	can crab, drained	115 mL
½ tsp.	dried tarragon	2 mL
1 tsp.	dried basil	5 mL
6	drops Tabasco	6
2 tbsp.	freshly grated Parmesan cheese	30 mL

Preheat oven to 350°F (180°C).

Blend the cream cheese and lemon juice until smooth. Add the crab, tarragon, basil and Tabasco and mix well. Put in a 3 x 5" (8 x 13 cm) ovenproof dish; sprinkle with Parmesan. (You can make this ahead to this point, cover and refrigerate, and add 5 minutes baking time.)

Bake for 15 minutes, until bubbly and lightly browned. Serve with assorted crackers.

CRAB AU GRATIN

**A partial make-ahead dish.
Serves 4-6 as a starter.**

You can substitute cooked boned cod or other firm white fish for the crab.

2 tbsp.	butter	30 mL
3 tbsp.	flour	45 mL
1 tsp.	dried basil	5 mL
1¾ cups	milk	425 mL
1 cup	grated sharp Cheddar	250 mL
1 tbsp.	sherry	15 mL
⅛ tsp.	cayenne pepper	0.5 mL
¼ tsp.	salt	1 mL
¼ tsp.	pepper	1 mL
2 x 4 oz.	cans crabmeat, drained	2 x 113 g
1 tbsp.	dry bread crumbs and/or grated Parmesan	15 mL

CRAB AU GRATIN
Continued.

Preheat oven to 350°F (180°C).

Melt the butter over medium heat. Add the flour and basil and stir for about 1 minute. Very slowly add the milk, stirring constantly until smooth after each addition. Continue stirring until the mixture begins to thicken slightly. Add the Cheddar, sherry, cayenne, salt and pepper and stir until the cheese is melted.

Divide the crab over bottoms of 4, 3 x 5" (7 x 13 cm) individual dishes, or 6 deep seafood shells. Pour the sauce over the crab. Sprinkle with crumbs and Parmesan. (You can make this ahead to this point, cover and refrigerate and add 5 minutes baking time.)

Bake for about 20-30 minutes, until bubbly and lightly browned.

ESCARGOT-STUFFED MUSHROOMS
A partial make-ahead dish.
Makes 36.

These can be messy if they're too hot or too big. Serve them as one-bite morsels, slightly warm, with a napkin, just in case.

36	mushrooms, about 1" (2.5 cm) diameter	36
¼ cup	butter	60 mL
3	garlic cloves, crushed	3
1	small can escargot (12-15 large), drained & chopped	1
¼ cup	minced sweet red pepper	60 mL
½ tsp.	pepper	2 mL

Preheat oven to 350°F (180°C).

Gently remove the stems from the mushrooms, scooping out a little extra to make a slightly bigger cavity. (Save stems for soup or stew.)

Melt the butter over medium-high heat, add the remaining ingredients and cook for about 5 minutes, stirring frequently. Stuff the escargot mixture into the mushroom cavities. (You can make this ahead to this point, cover and refrigerate, and add 5 minutes baking time.)

Place on a greased cookie sheet and bake for about 10 minutes. Let them cool slightly before serving, so they will be easier to handle.

ESCARGOT WITH WINE & BRANDY

A make-ahead dish.
Serves 4 as a starter.

This is a lighter version that many people find preferable to the usual butter-laden edition.

¼ cup	butter	60 mL
3	garlic cloves, crushed	3
¼ cup	finely chopped green onion	60 mL
1 tsp.	dried basil	5 mL
¼ tsp.	salt	1 mL
¼ tsp.	pepper	1 mL
2 tsp.	flour	10 mL
¾ cup	chicken broth	175 mL
6 oz.	can escargot (about 28 large), drained	170 mL
¼ cup	white wine	60 mL
1 tbsp.	brandy	15 mL

Melt the butter over low-medium heat. Add the garlic, onion, basil, salt and pepper and cook for about 5 minutes, stirring often.

Add flour and stir for 1 minute. Very slowly stir in the chicken broth, stirring constantly until smooth. Add the escargot and simmer gently, uncovered, about 5 minutes. Add the wine and brandy and simmer gently, uncovered, another 5 minutes. (This can be made ahead, covered and refrigerated, and reheated gently.)

To Serve: Put 6 or 7 escargot on each of 4 plates deep enough to hold some sauce, spoon some sauce over them and serve with lots of French bread to soak up the juices. These can also be served as finger food, using French bread cubes to pick up escargot and soak up some juices.

When adding liquid to a butter/flour combination, add it very slowly at first, stirring constantly to make a paste. As the mixture gets smooth, add a little more liquid and stir until creamy. This prevents the mixture from getting lumpy at the beginning. You can add liquid faster as you go along, but continue stirring until it thickens. Using a whisk instead of a spoon is a good idea too.

30

STEAMED MUSSELS IN WINE

A partial make-ahead dish.
Serves 4 as a starter.

In both mussel recipes, the broth is excellent — you'll wish you had more!

1 lb.	mussels	500 g
3 tbsp.	butter	45 mL
½	green pepper, finely chopped	½
½	small onion, finely chopped	½
6	large mushrooms, finely chopped	6
2	garlic cloves, crushed	2
1 tsp.	tarragon	5 mL
1 tsp.	basil	5 mL
¼ tsp.	pepper	1 mL
½ cup	chicken broth	125 mL
1 cup	white wine	250 mL

Clean the mussels, check that all are closed and set aside. If you are making the sauce ahead, clean the mussels just before finishing the dish.

Melt the butter over medium heat, add the green pepper, onion, mushrooms, garlic, tarragon, basil and pepper, and cook for about 10 minutes, stirring frequently. Add broth and wine, bring to low boil, and cook, uncovered, over medium heat for about 10 minutes. (You can make this ahead to this point, cover and refrigerate, and reheat gently.)

Increase heat to high, bring to a full boil, add the mussels and cover snugly. Cook for 4-5 minutes, until all the mussels are fully open. Discard any that do not open. Distribute broth and mussels evenly among 4 bowls. Serve with lots of French bread cubes to soak up the mussel broth.

Note: Buy mussels with closed shells or shells that close when pinched or tapped. Don't buy mussels with broken shells. Refrigerate mussels and use within 1 or 2 days. Wash mussels in several changes of water or under running water to remove any sand or mud. Ocean mussels have beards and river mussels are beardless. Remove beards before cooking.

STEAMED MUSSELS ITALIAN STYLE

A partial make-ahead dish.
Serves 4 as a starter.

These are so good, cook up a big batch of them for a cozy Friday night supper for two.

1 lb.	mussels	500 g
1 tbsp.	olive oil	15 mL
2	garlic cloves, crushed	2
1 tsp.	basil	5 mL
1 tsp.	oregano	5 mL
¼ cup	finely chopped onion	60 mL
¼ cup	finely chopped green pepper	60 mL
19 oz.	can tomatoes and the juice	540 mL
½ cup	white wine	125 mL

Clean the mussels, check that all are closed, and set aside. If you are making the sauce ahead, clean the mussels just before finishing the dish.

Heat the olive oil over medium heat, add the garlic, basil, oregano, onion and green pepper and cook for about 7 minutes, stirring frequently. Add the tomatoes, including the juice, and wine, bring to a full boil and cook over high heat for about 7 minutes, stirring often. (You can make this ahead to this point, cover and refrigerate, and reheat gently.)

Add the mussels, cover and cook for 4-5 minutes, until all the mussels are open. Discard any that do not open. Distribute broth and mussels evenly among 4 bowls. Serve with French bread cubes to soak up the juices.

See photograph on opposite page.

APPETIZERS

Steamed Mussels Italian Style, page 32
Wine Bread, page 53

SANGRIA UNO
Serves 8-10.

This is a light drink, for those who don't really like to drink much and for those who shouldn't! Sliced oranges make a nice garnish.

26 oz.	dry red wine	750 mL
6 oz.	port	170 mL
1	lime, sliced	1
1	lemon, sliced	1
16 oz.	7-Up (2 cups)	500 mL
16 oz.	club soda (2 cups)	500 mL

In a large glass bowl, combine wine, port, lime and lemon and let sit at room temperature, uncovered, for about 1 hour. Shortly before serving, add 7-Up and club soda. Serve over ice.

SANGRIA DOS
Serves 8-10.

This is a little heartier than Sangria Uno. If you want, just add a little soda water to weaken it and give it some fizz. Lemon and orange slices complement this nicely, also.

26 oz.	red wine	750 mL
8 oz.	port	250 mL
16 oz.	grape juice (2 cups)	500 mL
1 tbsp.	lime juice	30 mL
1	lime, cut into small chunks	1

In a large glass bowl, combine wine, port, grape juice, lime juice and lime. Let sit at room temperature, uncovered, for about 1 hour before serving. Serve over ice.

MULLED WINE
Serves 8.

There's nothing so heartwarming as a hot drink on a cold evening.

2 cups	apple juice	500 mL
26 oz.	red wine	750 mL
½ cup	sherry	125 mL
½ cup	liquid honey (more or less to taste)	125 mL
2	oranges, seeded, sliced	2
1	each, lime and lemon, seeded, sliced	1
2	cinnamon sticks	2
6	whole cloves	6

Combine everything in a 3-quart (3 L) glass pot. Cover and bring to a simmer over medium heat. Reduce heat to low; cook very gently for about 40 minutes. It should be hot and steaming, not boiling. Strain into mugs. If there is leftover wine, remove and discard solids. Otherwise, it becomes too pungent.

CHRISTMAS PUNCH
Serves 8-10.

Here's a pretty and tasty treat for kids and nondrinkers.

12 oz.	tin lemonade concentrate, partially thawed	341 mL
1 qt.	7-Up (regular or diet)	1 L
1 qt.	carbonated spring water	1 L
15 oz.	pkg. frozen sliced strawberries in light syrup, partially thawed	425 g

In a large punch bowl, combine lemonade, 7-Up and spring water until the lemonade has completely melted and dissolved. Stir in the strawberries until most of the slices have separated.

Variation: Add peeled, sliced kiwi for a festive look. You can also change the ratio of 7-Up to spring water to vary the sweetness.

SOUPS & BREADS

TOMATO SOUP
A make-ahead dish.
Serves 6 as a starter.

This is a very thick, very flavorful soup that was originally based on a French recipe. It's wonderful made with garden-fresh tomatoes, but you can enjoy it all year long.

6	large tomatoes, coarsely chopped	6
1 tbsp.	olive oil	15 mL
3	onions, minced	3
1	garlic head, cloves peeled (yes, the whole thing!)	1
2 tbsp.	sugar	30 mL
1 tsp.	salt	5 mL
1/2 tsp.	pepper	2 mL
1/4 cup	white wine	60 mL

Shake tomatoes in a colander for 30 seconds to remove some of the seeds.

Put the oil in a 3-quart (3 L) pot; add the onions, tomatoes and garlic. Cover and cook over medium heat, stirring occasionally, for about 20 minutes, until the onion is just a little tender.

Allow the soup to cool a few minutes, then process in a blender in several batches until almost smooth. (It will be a little pulpy.) Put the soup back into the pot, stir in the sugar, salt, pepper and white wine. Reheat on low-medium heat, and simmer very gently for about 10 minutes.

To Serve: Pour soup into individual bowls and garnish with a fresh sprig of parsley, basil, dill or other bright green herb.

CORN CHOWDER
A make-ahead dish.
Serves 6 as a starter.

This makes a nice thick chowder for a rainy day. For a thinner version, add another 1/2-1 cup (125-250 mL) water.

4	slices lean bacon, chopped, trim off fat, if you wish	4
1	onion, finely chopped	1
1	large potato, finely chopped	1
1/2 cup	water	125 mL
2 x 14 oz.	cans creamed corn	2 x 398 mL
1 cup	milk	250 mL
1/2 tsp.	curry powder	2 mL
1/2 tsp.	dry mustard	2 mL
1/4 tsp.	salt	1 mL
1/4 tsp.	pepper	1 mL

In a 3-quart (3 L) pot over medium-high heat, fry the bacon, onion and potato for about 10 minutes, stirring frequently. Slowly stir in the water. Cover, reduce heat to low-medium. Simmer about 8 minutes, stirring occasionally.

Add the remaining ingredients, bring to a simmer and cook for about 10 minutes, until potato is tender. Stir frequently because it has a tendency to stick to the bottom of the pot. (Can be made ahead, covered and refrigerated, and reheated gently.)

Note: For an easy supper on a long cold winter day, make this the night before, gently reheat and serve with lots of hearty bread and your favorite cheeses.

FRENCH ONION SOUP
A partial make-ahead dish.
Serves 4 as a starter.

A rich, hearty starter, and you don't need to love onions to love this soup.

2 tbsp.	butter	30 mL
2	large onions, very thinly sliced	2
1 tsp.	sugar	5 mL
1 tsp.	flour	5 mL
3 cups	beef broth	750 mL
1/2 tsp.	pepper	2 mL
1/2 tsp.	Worcestershire sauce	2 mL
2 tbsp.	sherry	30 mL
4	slices French bread	4
1 cup	grated Swiss cheese	250 mL
2 tbsp.	freshly grated Parmesan cheese	30 mL

Preheat oven to broil.

Melt the butter in a 3-quart (3 L) pot over low heat, add the onions and cook for about 20 minutes, stirring occasionally, until onions are soft and translucent. Add the sugar and stir for 1 minute; add the flour and stir for 1 minute. Very slowly, add the beef broth, stirring constantly until smooth. Add pepper and Worcestershire sauce. Cover and simmer for about 15 minutes. Stir in sherry. (You can make this ahead to this point and reheat gently.)

Pour the hot soup into ovenproof bowls, leaving about 3/4" (2 cm) headroom for the bread and cheese. Lay 1 slice of bread on top of the broth, sprinkle Swiss cheese over the bread and then sprinkle with the Parmesan. Broil in the oven until the cheese is lightly browned and bubbly.

BLACK BEAN SOUP
A make-ahead dish.
Serves 10-12 as a starter.

Be sure to test the beans for tenderness before you mash them. You may need to cook them longer depending on the hardness of your water and the age of the beans. It's better to cook a little longer than not long enough.

2 cups	dried black beans	500 mL
2 tbsp.-¼ cup	olive oil	30-60 mL
1 lb.	lean bacon, chopped, trim off fat, if you wish	500 g
8	garlic cloves, crushed	8
1	large onion, finely chopped	1
1	green pepper, finely chopped	1
5 cups	chicken broth	1.25 L
3 cups	water	750 mL
1 cup	red wine	250 mL
1	bay leaf	1
1 tbsp.	coriander or 2 tsp. (10 mL) curry powder	15 mL
1 tsp.	oregano	5 mL
2	1" (2.5 cm) dried red chili peppers	2
1	large lime, juice of (about 2 tbsp. [30 mL])	1

Soak beans overnight (at least 12 hours) in about 5 cups (1.25 L) of water.

Heat oil in a large pot, such as a Dutch oven, over medium-high heat. Add bacon, garlic, onion and green pepper; cook for about 15 minutes, stirring frequently.

Drain the beans and add them to the pot, along with the broth, water, wine, bay leaf, coriander, oregano and dried chili peppers. Bring to a simmer, cover and cook about 2½-3 hours, or longer if necessary, until beans are tender. Stir occasionally.

With a potato masher, mash the soup against the bottom of the pot until most of the beans are broken. Stir in the lime juice and keep the soup on low, low heat for about an hour, or longer. Remove chili peppers and bay leaf before serving. (This soup can be made ahead and reheated gently.)

An Attractive Garnish: Fill bowls with soup, put a 1-2 tbsp. (15-30 mL) dollop of sour cream in the center and sprinkle chopped chives over top.

MINESTRONE SOUP

A make-ahead dish.
Serves 8-10 as a starter.

Double the pasta and you could call this a stew! If you want a thinner version for a starter soup, reduce or omit the pasta.

1-2 tbsp.	olive oil	15-30 mL
4	garlic cloves, crushed	4
1 tsp.	dried oregano leaves	5 mL
1/2 tsp.	dried tarragon	2 mL
2	onions, finely chopped	2
3	celery stalks, finely chopped	3
1	green pepper, finely chopped	1
1	bay leaf	1
3 cups	chicken broth	750 mL
28 oz.	can tomatoes	796 mL
2 x 8"	zucchini, in 1/2" (1.3 cm) cubes	2 x 20 cm
1/2 cup	white wine	125 mL
1/4 cup	tiny pasta (alphabets, stars, etc.)	60 mL

In a 4-quart (4 L) pot over medium heat, heat the oil; add garlic, oregano, tarragon, onions, celery and green pepper and cook for about 8 minutes, stirring often until the vegetables start to soften. Add the bay leaf, broth and tomatoes. Cover and simmer gently for about 30 minutes.

Add the zucchini, cover and cook for about 20 minutes. Add the wine and pasta. Cover and simmer about 15 minutes, until pasta is tender. Remove the bay leaf before serving. (This can be made ahead and reheated gently.)

SHRIMP BISQUE

A make-ahead dish.
Serves 8 as a starter.

This is a lovely rich soup, the perfect introduction to an adults-only dinner party.

1 lb.	raw shrimp	500 g
2 cups	water	500 mL
¼ cup	butter	60 mL
2	garlic cloves, crushed	2
1	sweet red pepper, minced	1
3 cups	whole milk	750 mL
1 cup	35% cream (whipping cream)	250 mL
2 tbsp.	sherry	30 mL
¼ tsp.	cayenne	1 mL
½ tsp.	salt	2 mL

Peel the shrimp, and devein if desired. Put the shells in a small pot, add water, cover and bring to a low boil. Simmer for about 10 minutes. Strain and reserve the liquid and discard the shells.

Meanwhile, in a 4-quart (4 L) saucepan, melt the butter over medium heat, add the garlic and red pepper and sauté for about 5 minutes, stirring occasionally. Chop the shrimp and add to the red pepper mixture. Stir and cook for about 3 minutes, just until the shrimp meat is cooked.

Put the shrimp mixture into the blender, add 1 cup (250 mL) of milk and blend until almost smooth (it will be a little pulpy). Pour this back into the pot.

Over medium heat, slowly stir in 2 cups (500 mL) milk, then the liquid from the shells, then the cream and finally the sherry. Stir in the cayenne and salt and heat through, but do not boil. (This can be made ahead, covered and refrigerated, and reheated gently.)

To Serve: Garnish individual servings with a very thin slice of red pepper and/or a sprig of fresh basil.

MANHATTAN CLAM CHOWDER
A make-ahead dish.
Serves 10 as a starter.

*E*ach version of clam chowder has its fans. This tomato-based recipe is full of flavor and very colorful.

¼ lb.	lean bacon, chopped	125 g
1	onion, minced	1
1	green pepper, minced	1
2	large potatoes, peeled, in ½" (1.3 cm) cubes	2
½ tsp.	dried tarragon	2 mL
1 tsp.	bouquet garni	5 mL
2 x 5 oz.	cans clams, drained, liquid reserved	2 x 142 g
4 cups	Clamato juice	1 L
19 oz.	can tomatoes, chopped	540 mL

In a 4-quart (4 L) saucepan, over medium heat, cook the bacon for about 2 minutes. Add onion, green pepper and potatoes and cook for about 5 minutes, stirring often.

Stir in the tarragon, bouquet garni and drained clams for about 1 minute. Add the clam liquid, Clamato juice and tomatoes. Bring to a gentle boil. Cover and simmer for about 25-30 minutes, stirring occasionally, until potatoes are tender. (This can be made ahead, covered and refrigerated, and reheated gently.)

Note: Clamato juice is a delicious combination of tomato and clam flavors. If it is not available — use 3 cups (750 mL) of tomato juice and 1 cup (250 mL) of clam juice or try 2 cups (500 mL) tomato juice, 1½ cups (375 mL) V-8 juice and ½ cup (125 mL) red wine.

Variation: You can dress this up by adding 10-20 well scrubbed fresh raw clams during the last 10 minutes of cooking, until all the clams are fully opened. Put 1 or 2 clams in the center of each bowl.

See photograph on page 51.

NEW ENGLAND CLAM CHOWDER

A make-ahead dish.
Serves 6 as a starter.

An easy, healthy and hearty winter soup.

½ lb.	lean bacon, chopped	250 g
½	onion, finely chopped	½
1	carrot, finely chopped	1
2 tsp.	dried basil	10 mL
2 x 5 oz.	cans clams, drained, liquid reserved	2 x 142 g
4	potatoes, cut into ½" (1.3 cm) cubes	4
1 cup	chicken broth	250 mL
3 cups	whole milk, or use part 35% cream for a richer soup	750 mL
1	lemon, juice of (about 2 tbsp. [30 mL])	1
2 tbsp.	sherry or white wine	30 mL
¼ tsp.	salt	1 mL
¼ tsp.	pepper	1 mL
8 drops	Tabasco sauce	8 drops

In a 3-quart (3 L) pot, over medium-high heat, cook the bacon, onion, carrot and basil, stirring frequently, for about 5 minutes. Add the clam liquid (not the clams, yet), potatoes and chicken broth, and bring to a low boil. Cover and simmer for about 8 minutes, until the potatoes are almost tender.

Add the remaining ingredients, bring to a simmer, cover and cook over low heat for about 15 minutes, stirring occasionally so it doesn't stick to the bottom of the pot. If it seems too thick, add a little more milk. (This can be made ahead, covered and refrigerated, and reheated gently.)

Note: For a main course, this can feed four hungry people with the addition of some bread and cheese, or a hearty salad.

CURRIED CHICKEN SOUP

A make-ahead dish.
Serves 10 as a starter.

Although it has a spicy, hearty flavor, this great soup is very low in fat.

1 tbsp.	olive oil	15 mL
½ tsp.	sesame oil	2 mL
2	garlic cloves, crushed	2
4	slices of ginger (size of a quarter)	4
1-2	1" (2.5 cm) dried red chili peppers	1-2
2	carrots, minced	2
1	small onion, minced	1
4	celery stalks, minced	4
12 oz.	chicken cutlets or fillets, minced	340 g
1	sweet red pepper, minced	1
½ tbsp.	curry powder	7 mL
2 tbsp.	brown sugar	30 mL
7 cups	chicken broth	1.75 L

In a 4-quart (4 L) saucepan, heat the oils for about 30 seconds over medium heat, add the garlic, ginger, chili peppers, carrots, onion, celery and chicken and stir well. Cover and cook for about 15 minutes, stirring occasionally.

Add the red pepper and curry powder, cooking and stirring for about 3 minutes. Stir in the brown sugar and then the chicken broth. Bring to a simmer, reduce the heat to low, cover and cook for about 25-30 minutes, until the vegetables are tender. Remove the slices of ginger and the chili peppers before serving. (This can be made ahead, covered and refrigerated, and reheated gently.)

CROÛTONS
A make-ahead dish.
Makes about 2 cups (500 mL).

Homemade croûtons are so much better than store-bought. These are worth the trouble if you have the time to make them, and you can do that the day before.

4	1" (2.5 cm) thick slices French bread	4
2 tbsp.	olive oil	30 mL
2 tbsp.	commercially grated Parmesan	30 mL

Preheat oven to 300°F (150°C).

Remove and discard the crusts from the bread. Cut the bread into ½" (1.3 cm) pieces. Toss the bread with the oil and the Parmesan using a fork or your hands, so the bread soaks up most of the oil and cheese.

Spread out on a large greased cookie sheet and bake for about 10-15 minutes, until lightly browned, stirring occasionally. Let cool at room temperature. (These can be made ahead and kept, tightly covered, for a few days.)

To Serve: Serve with Caesar Salad, or another salad or soup in which you like croûtons.

Variations: Add 1 tsp. (5 mL) dried herbs, such as basil or oregano, or a crushed garlic clove to the cheese before adding the bread.

HERBED BREAD

A partial make-ahead dish.
Makes 12 slices.

This fancied-up store-bought bread tastes warm and wonderful.

1	French baguette	1
2	garlic cloves	2
¼ cup	butter, melted	60 mL
1 tbsp.	dried, crumbled oregano leaves	15 mL

Preheat oven to 350°F (180°C).

Slice baguette down the middle lengthwise and cut each half into about 6 pieces. Crush garlic into a small bowl; add butter and mix well. Using a pastry brush, brush garlic butter over the surface of the bread and sprinkle oregano over top. (Bread can be prepared up to this point earlier in the day, if covered closely so it does not dry out.)

Bake, uncovered, for about 10 minutes on an ungreased cookie sheet, just enough to heat through, but not enough to dry it out. Serve immediately.

ITALIAN BREAD

A partial make-ahead dish.
Makes 15-20 slices.

A very easy method of snazzing up bread, this is great with a salad.

1	loaf Italian or French bread	1
⅓ cup	olive oil	75 mL
2 tsp.	dried, crumbled oregano leaves	10 mL
½ tsp.	salt	2 mL
1½ cups	grated mozzarella	375 mL

Preheat oven to 350°F (180°C).

Slice loaf into about ¾" (2 cm) slices. Brush lightly with olive oil. Sprinkle oregano, salt and then mozzarella over top. (Bread can be prepared up to this point earlier in the day, if covered closely so it does not dry out.) Bake for about 10-15 minutes on an ungreased cookie sheet, until cheese melts and bubbles.

MEXICAN BRUSCHETTA

A partial make-ahead dish.
Makes 15-20 slices.

Great as an accompaniment to a luncheon or a light meal.

1	loaf French or Italian bread	
1/3 cup	olive oil	75 mL
1½ cups	grated Monterey Jack cheese	375 mL
1½ cups	Cozumel salsa, drained (page 15)	375 mL
	or chunky commercial salsa	

Preheat oven to broil.

Slice loaf into about ¾" slices. Brush lightly with olive oil and sprinkle the cheese over top. (This can be made earlier in the day if covered closely so the bread does not dry out.) Top with the salsa and broil until the cheese bubbles.

If you can't afford olive oil, canola oil is a good healthy alternative. However, the flavor is significantly different.

BASIL GARLIC BREAD
A make-ahead dish.
Makes 1 loaf.

A wonderful, easy bread that is great with pasta, or with just about anything, especially if you like basil and garlic.

2 cups	flour	500 mL
1 tsp.	salt	5 mL
2 tbsp.	sugar	30 mL
2 tsp.	baking powder	10 mL
¼ cup	chopped fresh basil	60 mL
½ cup	cold butter, cut up	125 mL
3	garlic cloves, crushed	3
1	egg, beaten	1
1 cup	milk	250 mL

Preheat oven to 350°F (180°C).

Combine flour, salt, sugar, baking powder and basil. Cut in butter until finely crumbled. Combine garlic, egg and milk and add to the flour mixture. Mix well. (Dough will be very sticky.) Spread in a lightly greased 4 x 8" (10 x 20 cm) loaf pan and bake for about 45 minutes.

See photograph on page 101.

SOUPS & BREADS

Manhattan Clam Chowder, page 44
Bruschetta, page 14
Red Leaf & Asiago Salad, page 60

WINE BREAD
A make-ahead dish.
Makes 1 loaf.

Wineries often serve their special wine bread recipes. Now you can make this Cheddar-wine version at home.

2 cups	flour	500 mL
2 tsp.	baking powder	10 mL
2 tbsp.	sugar	30 mL
1 tsp.	Bouquet Garni	5 mL
½ tsp.	salt	2 mL
1 cup	grated old Cheddar	250 mL
⅓ cup	cold butter, cut up	75 mL
½ cup	milk	125 mL
½ cup	white wine	125 mL
1	egg, beaten	1

Preheat oven to 350°F (180°C).

Combine flour, baking powder, sugar, Bouquet Garni, salt and Cheddar. Cut in butter until finely crumbled.

Combine milk, wine and egg and add to the flour mixture. Mix well. (Dough will be very sticky.) Spread in a lightly greased 4 x 8" (10 x 20 cm) loaf pan and bake for about 45 minutes.

Note: Bouquet Garni is a commercial mixture of herbs and spices. If you don't have it, use a combination of oregano, summer savory, marjoram, rosemary, basil, sage, thyme, dillweed and tarragon to equal 1 tsp. (5 mL) or try your own combination.

See photograph on page 33.

CHEESE BISCUITS

**A make-ahead dish.
Makes 15-20.**

Be sure to use a strong cheese, otherwise the cheesy flavor just fades into the other ingredients.

2 cups	flour	500 mL
1 tbsp.	baking powder	15 mL
1/2 tsp.	salt	2 mL
1/3 cup	cold butter	75 mL
1 cup	sharp Cheddar cheese, cut into 1/4" (1 cm) cubes	250 mL
1/4 cup	honey	60 mL
1/2 cup	plain yogurt	125 mL
1/4 cup	milk	60 mL

Preheat oven to 450°F (230°C).

Mix the flour, baking powder and salt. Add the butter and cut it in until grainy. Stir in the cubes of Cheddar.

Combine the honey, yogurt and milk and add to the flour mixture. Mix until a dough forms. Knead on a lightly floured surface for 1 minute.

Flatten dough to about 1/2" (1.3 cm) thickness. Cut with the top of a 3" (7 cm) glass and lay close together on a well-greased cookie sheet. Bake in the middle of the oven for about 12 minutes. You may have to scrape under the biscuits with a spatula to remove them because the cheese melts and makes the biscuits stick to the pan.

Variation: Add 1 tsp. (5 mL) dried herbs, such as oregano leaves or sweet basil, to the flour mixture to create Herbed Cheese Biscuits.

See photograph on page 119.

LOW-FAT BRAN MUFFINS
A make-ahead dish.
Makes 18.

Moist and fruit-filled, make these a "regular" part of your diet.

1 1/3 cups	bran	325 mL
1/2 cup	wheat germ	125 mL
1 1/2 cups	cake and pastry flour	375 mL
1/2 tsp.	salt	2 mL
1 tsp.	baking powder	5 mL
1 tsp.	baking soda	5 mL
1 cup	chopped dates	250 mL
1/2 cup	mashed banana	125 mL
1/2 cup	grated apple	125 mL
1/3 cup	molasses	75 mL
1/3 cup	corn syrup	75 mL
1 cup	skim milk	250 mL

Preheat oven to 400°F (200°C).

Combine the bran, wheat germ, flour, salt, baking powder, baking soda and dates.

In another bowl, mix the mashed banana, grated apple, molasses, corn syrup and skim milk, and then add to the dry ingredients. Mix until just blended. Divide the batter among 18 lightly greased or sprayed muffin cups. Bake for 12 minutes.

Variation: For the banana and grated apple you could substitute: 3/4 cup (75 mL) applesauce and another 1/2 cup (125 mL) flour.

LOW-FAT FRUIT MUFFINS

A make-ahead dish.
Makes 12.

These are low in fat but they really taste great.

1²/₃ cups	flour	400 mL
²/₃ cup	wheat germ	150 mL
1 tbsp.	baking powder	15 mL
¹/₂ tsp.	salt	2 mL
¹/₂ cup	finely chopped dried apricots	125 mL
¹/₂ cup	finely chopped pitted dates	125 mL
¹/₂ tsp.	cinnamon	2 mL
1¹/₂ cups	banana pulp (about 3 large bananas)	375 mL
1	egg, beaten	1
2 tbsp.	light olive oil (see note page 14)	30 mL
³/₄ cup	brown sugar	175 mL
¹/₃ cup	apple juice	75 mL

Preheat oven to 375°F (190°C).

Mix the flour, wheat germ, baking powder, salt, apricots, dates and cinnamon.

In another bowl, mix the banana pulp, egg, oil, sugar and apple juice. Add the liquid to the dry ingredients and mix until just blended. Divide the batter among 12 lightly greased or sprayed muffin cups. Bake for 20 minutes.

Variation: Substitute 1 cup (250 mL) applesauce for the oil and apple juice.

SALADS, DRESSINGS & SAUCES

TRADITIONAL FRENCH SALAD

A partial make-ahead dish.
Serves 6.

You can serve this salad after the main course, as they do in France, to clear the palate.

1	large head butter lettuce	1
3 tbsp.	extra virgin olive oil	45 mL
1 tbsp.	red wine vinegar	15 mL
1	garlic clove, crushed	1
¼ tsp.	salt	1 mL
¼ tsp.	pepper	1 mL
1 tsp.	Dijon mustard	5 mL

Clean and tear the lettuce into bite-sized pieces. Combine the oil, vinegar, garlic, salt, pepper and mustard in a jar and shake well. (You can make dressing ahead and refrigerate.)

Pour the dressing over the lettuce, toss gently, and let sit 5 minutes. Toss again and serve.

See photograph on back cover.

BUTTER LETTUCE & LIME DRESSING

A partial make-ahead dish.
Serves 8.

A very simple but tasty salad with lime, cumin and coriander dressing.

2	small limes, juice of (3 tbsp. [45 mL])	2
⅓ cup	olive oil	75 mL
1 tsp.	sugar	5 mL
½ tsp.	cumin	2 mL
½ tsp.	coriander	2 mL
2	heads butter lettuce, cleaned	2
½	red onion, thinly sliced	½

BUTTER LETTUCE & LIME DRESSING
Continued.

Combine the lime juice, olive oil, sugar, cumin and coriander in a jar and shake well. (The dressing can be made ahead and refrigerated.)

Tear the lettuce into bite-sized pieces. Combine it with the onion in a large bowl and toss well with the dressing.

See photograph on page 173.

See photograph on page 173.

BUTTER LETTUCE & VERMOUTH DRESSING
A partial make-ahead dish.
Serves 6.

There's no need to complicate things when you use butter lettuce — it's good even on its own.

1/3 cup	olive oil	75 mL
1 tbsp.	tarragon vinegar	15 mL
2 tbsp.	vermouth	30 mL
1/2 tsp.	dry mustard	2 mL
1 tsp.	sugar	5 mL
1/4 tsp.	salt	1 mL
1/4 tsp.	pepper	1 mL
1	large head butter lettuce, cleaned	1
2	large tomatoes, coarsely chopped	2
1/4	red onion, thinly sliced	1/4

Combine oil, vinegar, vermouth, mustard, sugar, salt and pepper in a jar and shake well. (The dressing can be made ahead and refrigerated.)

Tear the lettuce into bite-sized pieces. Put the lettuce, tomatoes and onions in bowl and toss well with the dressing.

Variation: If tarragon vinegar is not available, use 1 tbsp. (15 mL) red wine vinegar and 1/2 tsp. (2 mL) dried tarragon.

RED LEAF & ASIAGO SALAD

A partial make-ahead dish.
Serves 6.

These ingredients really work well together. The strong pungent flavors of balsamic vinegar and Asiago cheese are beautifully balanced by the olive oil and ripe tomatoes.

¼ cup	olive oil	60 mL
1 tbsp.	red wine vinegar	15 mL
1 tbsp.	balsamic vinegar	15 mL
½ tsp.	salt	2 mL
2 tsp.	sugar	10 mL
1 tsp.	dry mustard	5 mL
½ cup	finely chopped Asiago cheese (or another strong firm cheese, if you must)	125 mL
2 tbsp.	minced or ground crisply fried bacon	30 mL
¼ cup	sliced pimiento-stuffed green olives	60 mL
4	Roma tomatoes, chopped (or other tomatoes)	4
1	large head red or green leaf lettuce, cleaned	1

Mix the olive oil, vinegars, salt, sugar and mustard in a jar and shake well. (The dressing can be made ahead and refrigerated.) Combine the cheese, bacon, olives and tomatoes. (These can be prepared earlier, then covered and refrigerated until ready to use.)

Tear the lettuce into bite-sized pieces and put in a large bowl. About 5 minutes before serving, toss with the dressing, cheese, bacon, olives and tomatoes.

Variation: If balsamic vinegar is not available, use an extra tbsp. (15 mL) of red wine vinegar and ½ tsp. (2 mL) Worcestershire sauce.

See photograph on page 51.

RED LEAF & RADISHES

A partial make-ahead dish.
Serves 6.

Keep the radish slices very thin to match the delicacy of the red leaf lettuce.

¼ cup	olive oil	
2 tbsp.	balsamic vinegar (see variation page 60)	30 mL
¼ tsp.	salt	1 mL
¼ tsp.	ground marjoram or ½ tsp. (2 mL) oregano leaves	1 mL
1	head red leaf lettuce, cleaned	1
12	radishes, thinly sliced	12
⅓ cup	freshly grated Romano cheese	75 mL

Mix the oil, vinegar, salt and marjoram in a jar and shake well. (The dressing can be made ahead and refrigerated.)

Tear the lettuce into bite-sized pieces. Toss with the radishes and the dressing. Toss again with the cheese.

Prepare leafy lettuce for a salad earlier in the day. Wash leaves, discarding discolored pieces, and dry well. Place in a zip-lock bag, gently squeeze out all the air, and refrigerate until ready to use. The lettuce will keep quite well for several days.

ORANGE & ALMOND SALAD

A partial make-ahead dish.
Serves 6.

The addition of the sugared almonds gives this lovely salad a sweet and crunchy character.

¼ cup	olive oil	60 mL
1 tbsp.	raspberry or cider vinegar	15 mL
1 tbsp.	lemon juice	15 mL
2 tbsp.	orange juice	30 mL
1 tsp.	dried basil leaves	5 mL
1 tsp.	sugar	5 mL
¼ tsp.	salt	1 mL
¼ tsp.	pepper	1 mL
1 tsp.	butter	5 mL
¼ cup	sliced blanched almonds	60 mL
½ tsp.	sugar	2 mL
1	large head red or green leaf lettuce, cleaned	1
½	red onion, thinly sliced	½
2	oranges, peeled, seeded and chopped, or 10 oz. (284 mL) can mandarin oranges, drained	2

Mix the oil, vinegar, lemon juice, orange juice, basil, sugar, salt and pepper in a jar and shake well. (The dressing can be made ahead and refrigerated.)

Melt the butter in a small frying pan over medium-high heat, add the almonds and stir and cook for about 3 minutes, until lightly browned. Add the sugar and stir for about 30 seconds, until the sugar has melted and coated the almonds. Set aside to cool. (The sugared almonds can also be made ahead.)

Tear the lettuce into bite-sized pieces and put in a large bowl. Spread the onions and oranges over top.

About 5 minutes before serving, toss the salad with the dressing and sprinkle the almonds over top.

See photograph on page 137.

CAESAR SALAD CLASSIC
A partial make-ahead dish.
Serves 6.

Anchovies are usually a must for Caesar salad. However, for finicky eaters substitute about 1 tsp. (5 mL) chopped capers instead to get that slightly fishy flavor. Garlic lovers, use 4 cloves!

½ cup	olive oil	125 mL
1	egg yolk	1
1	lemon, juice of (about 2 tbsp. [30 mL])	1
2	garlic cloves, crushed, or more, to taste	2
½ tsp.	dry mustard	2 mL
2-4	anchovy fillets, minced (to taste)	2-4
½ tsp.	pepper	2 mL
¼ tsp.	salt	1 mL
¼ tsp.	Worcestershire sauce	1 mL
1	large head romaine lettuce, cleaned	1
¼	red onion, thinly sliced (optional)	¼
1 cup	croûtons (store-bought or see page 47)	250 mL
½ cup	freshly grated Parmesan cheese	125 mL

Combine the oil, egg yolk, lemon juice, garlic, mustard, anchovies, pepper, salt and Worcestershire sauce in a blender. Blend until smooth and creamy. (The dressing can be made ahead, covered and refrigerated.)

Tear the lettuce into bite-sized pieces. About 5 minutes before serving, toss the lettuce with the dressing and the onion, if using, for several minutes. Toss again with the croûtons and the Parmesan cheese.

Fresh Parmesan cheese may be more expensive than the commercially grated variety, but the taste difference is really incredible, and definitely justifies the price difference.

CAESAR SALAD – THE LIGHTER SIDE

A partial make-ahead dish.
Serves 6.

Although less rich than the classic recipe, this one is much lower in fat and a little quicker to make. Add some minced anchovies or a little anchovy paste if you have some.

¼ cup	olive oil	60 mL
1 tbsp.	lemon juice	15 mL
1	whole egg	1
2	garlic cloves, crushed	2
¼ tsp.	salt	1 mL
¼ tsp.	pepper	1 mL
2 tbsp.	light or no-fat sour cream	30 mL
1	large head Romaine, cleaned	1
⅓ cup	freshly grated Parmesan cheese	75 mL
2-3	slices bread, crusts removed, well toasted, cut into ½" (1.3 cm) pieces	2-3

Combine the oil, lemon juice, egg, garlic, salt, pepper and sour cream in a jar and shake well. (This can be made ahead and refrigerated.)

Tear the lettuce into bite-sized pieces. About 5 minutes before serving, toss the lettuce with the dressing for several minutes. Toss again with the croûtons and the cheese.

HONEY-MUSTARD DRESSING

A make-ahead recipe.
Makes about ½ cup (125 mL).

Here is a very easy salad dressing for when you're watching the scales.

⅓ cup	liquid honey	75 mL
2 tbsp.	prepared mustard (regular, hot dog variety)	30 mL
1	garlic clove, crushed	1
1 tbsp.	apple juice	15 mL

Put everything in a jar; shake well to mix completely, stirring the bottom of the jar once or twice. Use as a sweet dressing for salad.

CRUNCHY GREEN SALAD

With Raspberry Mustard Dressing
Marinating time is required. A partial make-ahead dish.
Serves 8.

This is a very crunchy, chewy marinated vegetable salad with some grated cheese and lettuce tossed in to lighten it up.

½ cup	olive oil	125 mL
2	garlic cloves, crushed	2
1 tsp.	dry mustard	5 mL
¼ tsp.	salt	1 mL
¼ cup	raspberry vinegar	60 mL
2	green peppers, slivered	2
1	small bunch green onions, chopped	1
3	celery stalks, chopped	3
2 cups	small broccoli florets	500 mL
1	large head Romaine lettuce, cleaned	1
¼ cup	freshly grated Parmesan cheese	60 mL

Combine the oil, garlic, mustard, salt and raspberry vinegar in jar and shake well.

Put the green pepper, onion, celery and broccoli in a glass bowl, add the dressing and toss well. Cover and refrigerate several hours or all day.

Remove from the refrigerator about 1 hour before serving. Tear the Romaine into bite-sized pieces. About 5 minutes before serving, toss with the vegetables and dressing, and then with the Parmesan cheese.

MIDDLE EASTERN SALAD

A partial make-ahead dish.
Serves 6.

A deliciously light salad that is just great with a Greek or Lebanese meal. Don't skimp on the feta — it really makes the difference.

1 tbsp.	tahini (sesame seed paste, also used in hommous)	15 mL
½	lemon, juice of (1 tbsp. [15 mL])	½
½ cup	yogurt	125 mL
1 tbsp.	water	15 mL
2	garlic cloves, crushed	2
1	head red-leaf lettuce	1
½	red onion, thinly sliced	½
1 cup	coarsely crumbled feta cheese (a must!)	250 mL

Combine the tahini, lemon juice, yogurt, water and garlic in a jar and shake well. (The dressing may be made ahead and refrigerated.)

Tear the lettuce into bite-sized pieces and put on plates, top with slices of red onion and then with crumbled feta. Spoon dressing over salad.

To make a simple salad more interesting, add some freshly grated feta or Parmesan cheese — a little goes a long way.

GREEK SALAD
A make-ahead dish.
Serves 6 as a side salad.

There is no lettuce in this authentic version of an old favorite.

1/3 cup	olive oil	75 mL
1/2	lemon, juice of (1 tbsp. [15 mL])	1/2
1 tsp.	dried oregano leaves	5 mL
1/2 tsp.	dried crumbled mint	2 mL
1/4 tsp.	salt	1 mL
1/4 tsp.	pepper	1 mL
1/4 tsp.	sugar	1 mL
1	large green pepper, in 1" (2.5 cm) pieces	1
1	sweet red pepper, in 1" (2.5 cm) pieces, (optional)	1
1/2	red onion, thinly sliced	1/2
1	English cucumber (about 10" [25 cm]), 1/2" (1.3 cm) chunks	1
3	firm, ripe tomatoes, coarsely chopped	3
2/3 cup	black olives	150 mL
4 oz.	feta cheese, in 1/2" (1.3 cm) chunks	115 g

Combine the oil, lemon juice, oregano, mint, salt, pepper and sugar in a jar and mix well. Put the vegetables in a bowl, pour the dressing over and mix well. Sprinkle the olives and feta cheese over top.

Serve close to room temperature. (This can be made ahead, covered and refrigerated until about 1 hour before serving.)

Variation: About 5 minutes before serving, toss the salad with 1 head of lettuce, washed and torn into bite-sized pieces. This will serve more people, or just add a different texture. Serve as a light lunch with crusty rolls.

See photograph on page 101.

Freeze leftover canned olives (sliced or whole) for use in other recipes, or to top off nachos or a salad.

ORIENTAL CHICKEN SALAD

A partial make-ahead dish.
Serves 4 as a lunch or light supper.

This has a wonderfully sweet and spicy flavor. It's less fuss than it seems if you get the chicken and the dressing ready the day before.

1 lb.	boneless chicken breast	500 g
2 tbsp.	peanut butter	30 mL
1 tbsp.	sherry	15 mL
1 tbsp.	honey	15 mL
1/2 tsp.	hot chili paste (e.g., sambal oelek)	2 mL
1 1/2 tsp.	water	7 mL
1/4 cup	olive oil	60 mL
1/2 tsp.	sesame oil	2 mL
2 tbsp.	Chinese-style soy sauce (light soy)	30 mL
2	garlic cloves, crushed	2
2 tbsp.	malt vinegar	30 mL
1	head romaine lettuce, cleaned	1
2	oranges, peeled, seeded and chopped	2
2	Roma tomatoes, sliced	2
2	celery stalks, thinly sliced	2
2	green onions, chopped	2

Preheat oven to broil.

Cut the chicken breast into fillets about 1 x 4" (2.5 x 10 cm). Mix the peanut butter, sherry, honey, hot chili paste and water. Add the chicken and stir to coat. Put the chicken fillets on a rack over a pan and broil, on the middle rack in oven, about 4 minutes per side, until just done and no longer pink in the middle. Let cool and slice into slivers.

Mix the olive oil, sesame oil, soy sauce, garlic and vinegar in a jar and shake well. Set aside. (You can make this ahead to this point, and cover and refrigerate the chicken and the dressing.)

Tear the lettuce into bite-sized pieces and put into a large bowl. Add the oranges, tomatoes, celery and onions. Toss with the dressing. Divide the lettuce mixture among 4 plates. Top with the chicken.

HOT THAI VEGETABLE SALAD

A partial make-ahead dish.
Serves 4.

An Indonesian classic, this Gado Gado version features a spicy peanut, chili pepper and coconut milk dressing.

2 tbsp.	olive oil	30 mL
3	1" (2.5 cm) dried red chili peppers	3
1 tbsp.	minced ginger	15 mL
2	garlic cloves, crushed	2
1 tbsp.	chopped fresh cilantro	15 mL
⅓ cup	peanut butter	75 mL
⅔ cup	coconut milk	150 mL
1 tbsp.	sherry	15 mL
1	lime, juice of (about 1½ tbsp. [22 mL])	1
4 cups	fresh vegetables (1" [2.5 cm] pieces of yellow, green and sweet red pepper, carrot matchsticks, thin celery slices, mushrooms pieces, small broccoli florets, thinly sliced onion, snow peas, etc.)	1 L
2 tbsp.	oil	30 mL

Heat olive oil over medium heat, add the chili peppers, ginger, garlic and cilantro and cook for 3 minutes, stirring often. Add the peanut butter and stir until well blended. Slowly stir in the coconut milk, sherry and lime juice. Bring to a gentle simmer and cook over low heat for about 5 minutes, stirring frequently. (The dressing can be made ahead, covered and refrigerated, and reheated gently.)

Meanwhile, heat a large frying pan for about 1 minute over high heat. Toss the vegetables with the 2 tbsp. (30 mL) of oil and add these to the hot frying pan, stirring constantly for about 3 minutes. Remove chili peppers. Divide the vegetables among 4 plates and spoon the hot dressing over the top.

Thai Shrimp and Veggies: To make Hot Thai Vegetable Salad (see above) into a main course, simply add 1 lb. (500 g) large peeled shrimp to the vegetables and cook just until shrimp are pink all over. Toss with the hot dressing and serve over rice vermicelli.

See photograph on the front cover.

SPICY INDONESIAN SALAD

A make-ahead dish.
Serves 8.

You can serve this right away or make it the day before and refrigerate. Let it come close to room temperature before serving.

¼ cup	olive oil	60 mL
3 tbsp.	peanut butter	45 mL
1 tsp.	sesame oil	5 mL
2 tbsp.	minced ginger	30 mL
2	garlic cloves, crushed	2
¼ cup	lime juice	60 mL
3	1" (2.5 cm) dried red chili peppers (or less)	3
2 tbsp.	brown sugar	30 mL
¼ cup	Chinese soy sauce	60 mL
6 oz.	rice vermicelli or rice stick	170 g
1	small carrot	1
3"	piece English cucumber	7 cm
½	green pepper	½
½	sweet red pepper	½
2 tbsp.	minced peanuts	30 mL

Combine the oil, peanut butter, sesame oil, ginger, garlic, lime juice, chili peppers, sugar and soy sauce in a blender and blend until smooth. (Makes about 1 cup [250 g].)

Put the rice vermicelli into a pot, cover with boiling water, cover and leave 15 minutes.

Cut the carrot, cucumber, green pepper and red pepper into match-stick pieces. Toss the vegetables with about ⅓ of the dressing.

Drain the vermicelli and rinse lightly with hot water. Pour the remaining dressing over and toss gently. Top with the dressing and vegetables. Sprinkle peanuts over top. (This can be made ahead, covered and refrigerated until about 2 hours before serving.)

VARIATION: If you want to use this as a starter salad for a dinner party, line bowls (up to 12) with some lettuce leaves, top the lettuce with the noodle/vegetable mixture, and let sit for about 10 minutes. (I have left this for over an hour and it's still fine!)

PASTA VEGETABLE SALAD

A make-ahead dish.
Serves 8 as a side dish.

This is great for a barbecue, especially if you have to take it to someone else's house. It's easy, it's portable and it tastes great.

8 oz.	rotini or similar pasta	250 g
1/3 cup	olive oil	75 mL
2	garlic cloves, crushed, or more, to taste	2
1 tsp.	dried oregano leaves	5 mL
1/2 tsp.	dried mint	2 mL
2	limes, juice of (about 3 tbsp. [45 mL])	2
1 tsp.	sugar	5 mL
1	sweet red pepper, slivered	1
2	green peppers, slivered	2
1/2	red onion, thinly sliced	1/2
1	cucumber, peeled, seeded, in 1/2" (1.3 cm) cubes	1
6 oz.	feta cheese, in 1/3" (8 mm) cubes	170 g
1/2 cup	sliced black olives	125 mL

Cook the rotini until tender. Rinse in hot water and then in cold water.

Meanwhile, mix the olive oil, garlic, oregano, mint, lime juice and sugar in a jar and shake well. Toss the dressing with the pasta, red and green peppers, onion and cucumber. Top with the feta and olives. Serve at close to room temperature. (This can be made ahead, covered and refrigerated until about 1 hour before serving.)

See photograph on page 119.

LIGHT & ZESTY PASTA SALAD

A make-ahead dish.
Serves 6 as a side dish.

Less oil, but not less taste!

8 oz.	rotini or similar pasta	250 g
2	oranges, juice of (about ⅓ cup [75 mL])	2
1 tbsp.	Dijon mustard	15 mL
1-2	limes, juice of (about 2 tbsp. [30 mL])	1-2
1 tbsp.	olive oil	15 mL
1 tbsp.	sugar	15 mL
½ tsp.	Worcestershire sauce	2 mL
½	green pepper, slivered	½
½	small red onion, thinly sliced	½
⅓	English cucumber, in ½" (1.3 cm) cubes	⅓
½ cup	grated feta cheese	125 mL

Cook the pasta until just tender, drain and rinse it in hot and then cold water.

Meanwhile, mix the orange juice, mustard, lime juice, olive oil, sugar and Worcestershire sauce. Toss the pasta, dressing and vegetables together. Top with the feta. Serve at close to room temperature. (This can be made ahead, covered and refrigerated until about 1 hour before serving.)

To slice an onion safely, cut it in half from top to bottom first, put cut side down, and then slice across the grain. For full rings, cut a small section off one side, lay the onion with the cut section flat on the counter, and slice towards the center from each end, finishing with the middle of the onion.

To counteract the tear-making properties of onion, some people advise soaking them in cold water for 5 minutes and peeling them under cold running water. Another method is to hold a slice of bread under your chin while you peel and chop onions. The bread absorbs the odor.

MARINATED ONIONS

Marinating time is required. A make-ahead dish. Serves 8.

This is a great accompaniment at a barbecue.

1 cup	cider vinegar	250 mL
1 cup	apple juice	250 mL
2 tsp.	salt	10 mL
½ cup	white sugar	125 mL
¼ tsp.	pepper	1 mL
½ tsp.	ground dried marjoram	2 mL
1	large white onion, very thinly sliced	1
1	large red onion, very thinly sliced	1
1	bunch green onions, chopped	1

Mix the vinegar, apple juice, salt, sugar, pepper and marjoram in a glass dish. Add the onions and mix well. Cover and refrigerate at least overnight, or up to several days. Drain well and serve.

TOMATO & ARTICHOKE SALAD

A make-ahead dish. Serves 4-6.

This truly is better with a top quality olive oil. It adds wonderful flavor.

¼ cup	extra-virgin olive oil	60 mL
1 tbsp.	red wine or balsamic vinegar	15 mL
¼ tsp.	salt	1 mL
¼ tsp.	pepper	1 mL
½ tsp.	dried oregano leaves	2 mL
14 oz.	can artichoke hearts, drained and quartered	398 mL
4	ripe tomatoes, coarsely chopped	4
¼ cup	finely chopped green onion	60 mL

Combine the oil, vinegar, salt, pepper and oregano and mix well in a glass bowl. Add the artichokes, tomatoes and onion and stir gently. Serve close to room temperature. (This can be made ahead, covered and refrigerated until about 1 hour before serving.)

PARSLEY & TOMATO SALAD

A make-ahead dish.
Serves 6.

Parsley, so often discarded as a restaurant garnish, actually makes a great salad. Try this one, or order a Tabbouleh Salad the next time you're in a Lebanese restaurant.

1	bunch parsley, stems discarded, leaves coarsely chopped	1
3	large ripe tomatoes, coarsely chopped	3
1/2	white or red onion, thinly sliced	1/2
1/3 cup	sliced black olives	75 mL
1/3 cup	olive oil	75 mL
1	lemon, juice of (about 2 tbsp. [30 mL])	1
2 tbsp.	red wine vinegar	30 mL
1 tsp.	dried mint	5 mL
1 tsp.	coriander	5 mL
1/2 tsp.	cumin	2 mL
2	garlic cloves, crushed, or more, to taste	2
1/4 tsp.	salt	1 mL
1/4 tsp.	pepper	1 mL
1/4 cup	grated feta cheese	60 mL

Combine the parsley, tomatoes, onion and black olives in a bowl.

Mix the oil, lemon juice, vinegar, mint, coriander, cumin, garlic, salt and pepper in a jar and shake well. Toss with the vegetables. Sprinkle with the feta cheese. Serve close to room temperature. (This can be made ahead, covered and refrigerated until about 1 hour before serving.)

Variation: Instead of coriander and cumin, use 1/2 tsp. (2 mL) each cinnamon and curry powder.

PARSLEY & CHICK-PEA SALAD

A make-ahead dish.
Serves 6.

Lemon and cilantro infuse this salad with the most pleasing fresh taste!

19 oz.	can chick-peas, drained	540 mL
2 cups	chopped fresh parsley	500 mL
¼ cup	minced red or green onion	60 mL
¼ cup	minced green or sweet red pepper	60 mL
¼ cup	packed chopped fresh cilantro	60 mL
¼ cup	olive oil	60 mL
1-2	lemons, juice of (about 3 tbsp. [45 mL])	1-2

Combine all ingredients in a glass bowl and stir well. Serve close to room temperature. (This can be made ahead, covered and refrigerated for 2 days.)

CHICK-PEA & BEAN SALAD

A make-ahead dish.
Serves 6-8.

With this salad, you can really be prepared and make it the day before.

¼ cup	olive oil	60 mL
2 tbsp.	tarragon vinegar (see Variation, page 59)	30 mL
½ tsp.	salt	2 mL
1 tsp.	dry mustard	5 mL
1 tbsp.	honey	15 mL
2	garlic cloves, crushed	2
14 oz.	can kidney beans, drained	398 mL
19 oz.	can chick-peas, drained	540 mL
14 oz.	can baby corn, drained and halved	398 mL
¼ cup	each minced green pepper, red onion, celery	60 mL

Combine the oil, vinegar, salt, mustard, honey and garlic in a glass bowl and mix well. Add the rest of the ingredients and stir gently. Serve at close to room temperature. (This can be made ahead, covered and refrigerated until about 1 hour before serving.)

FRESH POTATO SALAD

A make-ahead dish.
Serves 6.

Small new white potatoes and fresh garden herbs makes this a truly refreshing potato salad.

2 lbs.	small (egg-sized) new potatoes, unpeeled	1 kg
1	sweet red pepper, in ½" (1.3 cm) pieces	1
⅓ cup	thinly sliced red onion	75 mL
3 tbsp.	olive oil	45 mL
1 tbsp.	raspberry or tarragon or red wine vinegar	15 mL
1-2 tbsp.	(packed) chopped fresh oregano	15-30 mL
1-2 tbsp.	(packed) chopped fresh basil	15-30 mL
2	garlic cloves, crushed	2
¼ tsp.	salt	1 mL
¼ tsp.	pepper	1 mL

Cover the whole potatoes with water and boil until just tender. (Do not overcook or the salad will be mushy.) Drain potatoes and cut into 2-3 pieces each. Put into a glass bowl with the peppers and the onion.

Combine the oil, vinegar, oregano, basil, garlic, salt and pepper. Shake well in a jar. Pour over the vegetables and mix gently but well. Serve at close to room temperature. (This can be made ahead, covered and refrigerated until about 1 hour before serving.)

SWEET MANGO CHUTNEY
A make-ahead dish.
Makes 9, 12 oz. (340 g) jars.

Chutney is the perfect accent for curry dishes. It is also very good with sharp cheeses or cream cheese. If you like a very hot chutney, crush some of the dried red chilies. Also, if you are nervous about shelf life, you may want to process these using the hot water canner method.

3 cups	cider vinegar	750 mL
1 cup	white vinegar	250 mL
3 cups	brown sugar	750 mL
12	ripe (not overripe) mangos, peeled and chopped in 1/2" (1.3 cm) pieces	12
1/4 cup	grated fresh ginger	60 mL
2 tbsp.	crushed fresh garlic	30 mL
1 tbsp.	cinnamon	15 mL
1 tbsp.	cumin	15 mL
1 tbsp.	coriander	15 mL
8	1" (2.5 cm) dried red chili peppers	8
2 cups	seedless raisins	500 mL

In a large pot, heat the vinegars and sugar over high heat until the mixture just starts to bubble. Add everything else and stir well. Reduce the heat to medium and bring to a simmer. Continue cooking for about 1 hour, stirring often. Remove whole chili peppers before bottling.

Put into hot sterilized jars and let cool until they can be held with the bare hands. Melt some paraffin wax and pour a very thin film over the surface of the chutney. Let set for about 30 minutes. Pour another thin film of wax over top and swirl it around to ensure the whole surface is sealed. Let set for 30 minutes. Cover with lids and rings and store in a cool dark place.

Hint: Be sure the chutney comes up to the bottom of the rim of the jar. Otherwise, when you are trying to remove the wax, you will have to dig under the rim to get it out and you will end up with some bits of wax in your chutney.

See photograph on page 137.

MINT SAUCE

A make-ahead sauce.
Makes about 1 cup (250 mL).

This is a very easy sauce that goes well with lamb and in a variety of Greek and other recipes.

¼ cup	water	60 mL
2 tbsp.	sugar	30 mL
½ cup	chopped fresh mint, or 2 tbsp. [30 mL] dried	125 mL
¼ cup	white wine	60 mL
¼ cup	cider vinegar	60 mL

In a small pot, bring the water to a boil; add the sugar and stir for about 1 minute, until dissolved. Add the mint, wine and vinegar. Stir well and bring to a boil. Immediately remove from heat. Let cool and store in a jar in the refrigerator until ready to use.

Note: Mint is a symbol of hospitality. Peppermint and spearmint are the most popular of the 30 plus varieties available. Grow your own mint in a separate area in your garden (it is very aggressive and tends to take over). Try some of the fruit-scented mints (apple, orange, pineapple or lemon), finely chopped, in honey or in sauces. They add great flavor to fresh fruit salads.

VEGETABLES & RICE DISHES

BAKED TOMATOES
A partial make-ahead dish.
Serves 4.

These are so simple, yet pretty and flavorful.

4	ripe tomatoes, stems removed, halved	4
2 tbsp.	olive oil	30 mL
2 tbsp.	freshly grated Parmesan cheese	30 mL
2	garlic cloves, crushed	2
1/4 tsp.	pepper	1 mL
1/2 tsp.	ground oregano	2 mL

Preheat oven to 350°F (180°C).

Lay the 8 tomato halves flat on a cookie sheet. Mix the rest of ingredients well and spread on top of the tomatoes. (You can make this ahead to this point, cover and refrigerate, and add 5 minutes baking time.)

Bake for about 15 minutes; increase heat to broil and broil until tops are lightly browned and bubbly.

MINTED PEAS
Serves 4-6.

These go well with leg of lamb.

2 cups	fresh or frozen peas	500 mL
2 tbsp.	butter	30 mL
2 tbsp	chopped fresh mint or 1 tsp. (5 mL) crumbled dry mint	30 mL

In a 1-quart (1 L) pot, cover fresh peas with water; cover and bring to a low boil. Simmer about 7-10 minutes, or until tender. (If using frozen peas, boil them for about 3 minutes in 1/2 cup [125 mL] water.) Drain. Add the butter and mint and stir well. Cover and let sit on very low heat about 2 minutes. Stir and serve.

GINGERED BROCCOLI
Serves 4-6.

Be careful not to overcook the broccoli. Serve it tender crisp and bright green.

1 lb.	broccoli, tough stems removed, divided into large florets	500 g
2 tbsp.	butter	30 mL
1 tbsp.	minced fresh ginger	15 mL

In a large pot, bring about ½" (1.3 cm) water to a full boil. Add the broccoli; cover and boil for about 3 minutes, until just slightly tender. Be careful not to let the pot boil dry. Steam the broccoli if you prefer.

Meanwhile, melt butter over medium-high heat in a large frying pan. Add the ginger and cook for about 1 minute. Add the drained broccoli and stir well, cover and cook for 1 minute. Stir again and serve.

SPINACH IN BUTTER SAUCE
Serves 4-6.

This may seem like a lot of spinach, but once cooked it will be just a fraction of its original bulk.

2	large bunches spinach	2
¼ cup	butter	60 mL
2 tsp.	lemon juice	10 mL

Clean the spinach well and discard any large stems. Melt the butter in a pot just large enough to squeeze in all the spinach. Add the lemon juice and stir; add the spinach with just the water that clings to its leaves; cover and bring to a boil. Cook just until the spinach is fully wilted, about 2-3 minutes. Be careful that not all the liquid evaporates. This will depend on the type of pots you have. If the bottom of the pot seems dry, add 1 tbsp. (15 mL) of water.

GREEN BEANS WITH SUGARED ALMONDS
Serves 6.

Sugared almonds add a sweet crunchy texture to this dish.

1 lb.	green beans	500 g
2 tbsp.	butter	30 mL
½ cup	sliced blanched almonds	125 mL
1 tsp.	sugar	5 mL

Trim and discard the ends of the beans. Bring about 1" (2.5 cm) of water to a boil in a medium-sized pot. Add the beans and cover. Boil for about 8-10 minutes, depending on the size and age of the beans, until tender.

Meanwhile, in a large frying pan, melt the butter over medium-high heat. Add the almonds and cook for about 3 minutes, until lightly browned. Stir often so the almonds will not scorch. Add the sugar and stir and cook for about 30 seconds, until sugar melts and coats the almonds. Drain the beans; put on a platter; sprinkle with almonds.

SAUTÉED ZUCCHINI AND TOMATOES
Serves 6.

A very simple and colorful side vegetable that's packed with flavor.

2 tbsp.	olive oil	30 mL
3	garlic cloves, crushed, or more, to taste	3
1 tsp.	dried oregano leaves	5 mL
1 tsp.	dried basil	5 mL
2	1" (2.5 cm) dried red chili peppers	2
½	onion, finely chopped	½
3	8" (20 cm) zucchini, ⅓" (3 mm) slices	3
4	large tomatoes, chopped	4
	freshly grated Parmesan or Romano cheese, if desired	

SAUTÉED ZUCCHINI AND TOMATOES
Continued.

In a large frying pan, over medium heat, cook the oil, garlic, oregano, basil, chili peppers and onion for about 3 minutes. Add the zucchini; stir well. Cover and cook for about 5 minutes, stirring occasionally.

Toss the tomatoes in a colander for about 30 seconds; add to the zucchini. Reduce the heat to medium-low and simmer, uncovered, for about 15 minutes, until most of the excess liquid has evaporated, stirring occasionally. Remove chili peppers before serving. Serve with freshly grated Parmesan or Romano cheese, if desired.

BAKED STUFFED ZUCCHINI
A partial make-ahead dish.
Serves 6.

Two of these on a plate take up a lot of space, so plan accordingly.

6	6" (15 cm) zucchini, ends trimmed	6
2 tbsp.	olive oil	30 mL
2	garlic cloves, crushed	2
¼ tsp.	each salt and pepper	1 mL
2 tsp.	dried oregano leaves	10 mL
3	large tomatoes, chopped	3
½ cup	fresh fine bread crumbs	125 mL
⅓ cup	freshly grated Parmesan cheese	75 mL

Preheat oven to 350°F (180°C).

Halve the zucchini lengthwise and scoop out the seeds to create a slight indentation, about ¼" (1 cm) deep. Set aside.

In a medium-sized frying pan, heat the oil over medium-high heat; add the garlic, salt, pepper and oregano. Stir and cook for about 1 minute. Add the tomatoes and cook for about 5 minutes, stirring often. Stir in the bread crumbs. Spoon the filling evenly into the zucchini "boats" and sprinkle Parmesan cheese on top. (You can make this ahead to this point, cover and refrigerate, and add 5 minutes baking time.)

Bake on an ungreased cookie sheet for 20 minutes.

RATATOUILLE MEDITÉ
A partial make-ahead dish.
Serves 8 as a side vegetable.

This very popular dish from Provence can also be served warm or cold as an appetizer with crisp crackers or baguette slices. For a luncheon, divide the mixture into 6 individual ramekins, top with some grated cheese, bake for about 30 minutes, and serve with bread and salad.

1 tbsp.	olive oil	15 mL
3	garlic cloves, crushed	3
1½ tsp.	oregano leaves	7 mL
½ tsp.	salt	2 mL
1	large green pepper, in 1" (2.5 cm) pieces	1
1	small onion, in ½" (1.3 cm) pieces	1
1	eggplant, in 1" (2.5 cm) pieces	1
1	8" zucchini, in ½" (1.3 cm) pieces	1
½ cup	½" (1.3 cm) cubes mozzarella cheese	125 mL
19 oz.	can tomatoes	540 mL

Preheat oven to 350°F (180°C).

In a 4-quart (4 L) casserole, heat the oil over medium heat; add the garlic, oregano, salt, green pepper and onion. Cook for about 10 minutes, stirring occasionally.

Add eggplant, zucchini, cheese and tomatoes and stir well. (You can make this ahead to this point, cover and refrigerate, and add 5-10 minutes baking time.)

Cover and bake for 40 minutes.

To take a lot of the last minute preparation out of recipes that call for chopped onion, peppers, broccoli, cauliflower, carrots, etc., clean and chop vegetables and seal in airtight bags early in the day or even the day before. This makes stir-fries and many other "last minute" recipes into partial make-ahead dishes.

RED CABBAGE AND RUTABAGA
Serves 6.

Do something nice to your winter vegetables!

¼ cup	butter	60 mL
1½-2 lbs.	red cabbage, grated	750 g-1 kg
1½-2 lbs.	rutabaga or turnip, grated	750 g-1 kg
¼ cup	brown sugar	60 mL
½ tsp.	salt	2 mL

In a large frying pan, melt butter over low heat. Add remaining ingredients and mix well. Cover and cook for about 25 minutes, stirring frequently.

CARROTS PARMESAN
Serves 4-6.

Carrots with a light cheesy coating.

6	carrots, peeled and sliced, ¼" (1 cm) coins	6
2 tbsp.	lemon juice	30 mL
⅓ cup	freshly grated Parmesan cheese	75 mL

In a 2-quart (2 L) pot, cover the carrots with water; cover and bring to a boil. Cook for about 15-20 minutes, until tender. Reduce heat to low.

Drain the carrots; add the lemon juice and Parmesan and stir well. Cover and let sit on low heat for about 1 minute, until Parmesan is melted. Stir and serve.

GARLICKY CARROTS
Serves 4-6.

Butter and garlic can make even carrots taste rich.

6	carrots, peeled and sliced, ¼" (1 cm) diagonals	6
2 tbsp.	butter	30 mL
2	garlic cloves, crushed	2
¼ tsp.	salt	1 mL
¼ tsp.	pepper	1 mL
1 tbsp.	sherry or white wine	15 mL

In a 2-quart (2 L) pot, cover the carrots with water; cover and bring to a boil. Cook for about 15-20 minutes, until tender.

Meanwhile, in a large frying pan, melt the butter over low heat; add the garlic, salt and pepper, and cook for about 3 minutes. Add the sherry and cook for about 2 minutes. Add the drained carrots; stir well and heat through, covered, about 2 minutes.

LEMONY CARROTS
Serves 4-6.

A fresh and zesty lemony flavor.

6	carrots	6
2 tbsp.	butter	30 mL
2 tbsp.	lemon juice	30 mL

Cut the carrots into 2" (5 cm) lengths and halve or quarter them lengthwise, depending on the thickness of the carrots. In a 2-quart (2 L) pot cover the carrots with water; cover and bring to a boil. Cook for about 15-20 minutes, until tender.

Drain the carrots, add the butter and lemon juice and stir well. Let sit on low heat, covered, about 2 minutes. Stir well and serve.

NEWFOUNDLAND TURNIP BAKE

A partial make-ahead dish.
Serves 4-6.

This is a good winter vegetable dish, warm and comforting.

1	turnip (about 3-4" [7-10 cm] diameter)	1
4	carrots	4
¼ cup	brown sugar	60 mL
2 tbsp.	butter	30 mL
½ tsp.	salt	2 mL
½ tsp.	cinnamon	2 mL
½-1 cup	water (from the boiled vegetables)	125-250 mL
1 tsp.	butter	5 mL

Peel and chop the turnip and carrots into 1" (2.5 cm) pieces. Put in a 3-quart (3 L) pot; cover with water and bring to a boil. Cover and cook for about 30 minutes, until very tender. Drain the vegetables, saving about 1 cup (250 mL) of the water.

Preheat oven to 350°F (180°C).

Mash the vegetables, add the sugar, the 2 tbsp. butter, salt, cinnamon and enough water to give the consistency of mashed potatoes. Mix well. Put in a 3-quart (3 L) casserole and dot in several places with the 1 tsp. (5 mL) butter. (You can make this ahead to this point, cover and refrigerate, and add 5 minutes baking time.)

Bake, uncovered, for about 20 minutes.

During the winter, if carrots look and taste old, add 1-2 tbsp. (15-30 mL) of sugar to the cooking water to refresh them.

CHINESE VEGETABLE MEDLEY

Serves 4.

Be sure to keep the potato pieces small or they won't be ready when the peppers are cooked.

1 tbsp.	olive oil	15 mL
2 tbsp.	rice or cider vinegar	30 mL
1 tsp.	sesame oil	5 mL
4	slices ginger, the size of a quarter	4
2	garlic cloves, crushed	2
3	potatoes, in 1/3" (8 mm) cubes (no bigger!)	3
1	green pepper, 1" (2.5 cm) pieces	1
1	red pepper, 1" (2.5 cm) pieces	1
1/2	onion, in 1/2" (1.3 cm) wide wedges, separated	1/2

Preheat oven to 350°F (180°C).

Mix the oil, vinegar, sesame oil, ginger and garlic in a 2-quart (2 L) casserole. Add the vegetables and mix well to coat. Bake, uncovered, for 50-60 minutes, stirring occasionally. Remove ginger before serving.

ROAST MINTED POTATOES

Serves 6-8.

Ideally, most of the liquid will be absorbed or evaporated and the edges of the potatoes will get a little crunchy.

6	large potatoes (about 3 x 5" [7 x 13 cm])	6
1/4 cup	olive oil	60 mL
1 tsp.	dried mint	5 mL
1/4 cup	lemon juice	60 mL

ROAST MINTED POTATOES
Continued.

Preheat oven to 350°F (180°C).

Peel and quarter the potatoes. Toss with the rest of the ingredients. Put in a 9 x 13" (23 x 33 cm) casserole and bake, uncovered, for about 1 hour, until tender, stirring gently several times.

Variation: Basil and Tarragon Roasted Potatoes: Prepare as for Roast Minted Potatoes, except use 1 tbsp. (15 mL) dried basil or 1/4 cup (60 mL) chopped fresh basil instead of mint, and 1/4 cup (60 mL) tarragon vinegar instead of lemon juice.

BAKED "FRIES"
Serves 4.

Six potatoes should serve four people, but you may want to put on a few extra, just in case. If you prefer, leave the peel on the potatoes for extra flavor and nutrition.

6	potatoes (about 2" (5 cm) in diameter, 3-4" [7-10 cm] long)	6
1 tbsp.	olive oil	15 mL
1 tsp.	sesame oil	5 mL
1 tsp.	dried oregano leaves	5 mL
1/2 tsp.	pepper	2 mL
1/2 tsp.	salt	2 mL

Preheat oven to 400°F (200°C).

Peel the potatoes, if you wish, and cut each into about 3 flat wide slices, about 1/2" (1.3 cm) thick. Rinse and drain well and put into a large bowl. Pour the olive oil and sesame oil over the potato slices and toss to coat. Spread the slices in a single layer on 1 or 2 shallow pans. Sprinkle oregano and pepper over potatoes, and bake for about 30 minutes. Sprinkle with the salt.

Variation: Try other herbs and spices instead of oregano or maybe sprinkle with grated cheese.

STUFFED FETA POTATOES

A partial make-ahead dish.
Serves 4.

These are a nice change from baked potatoes, and you won't need to have the usual condiments (sour cream, butter, chives, etc.) on the table at serving time.

4	large potatoes	4
2 oz.	feta cheese, grated	55 g
1/2 cup	yogurt	125 mL
1/2 tsp.	dillweed	2 mL
1/4 cup	milk	60 mL

Preheat oven to 425°F (200°C).

Bake cleaned unpeeled potatoes for about 40 minutes, until a knife slides in and out easily. Remove from oven. Reduce heat to 375°F (190°C).

Cut the potatoes in half lengthwise. (You may want to wear an oven mitt). Gently scoop out the middle and around the sides without tearing the jacket. Whip the scooped-out potato pulp with the rest of the ingredients until fairly smooth. Put the stuffing back into the potato skins. (You can make this ahead to this point, cover and refrigerate, and add an extra 5 minutes baking time.)

Bake at 375°F (190°C) for about 15 minutes, to heat through and melt the cheese.

STUFFED CHEDDAR POTATOES

A partial make-ahead dish.
Serves 4.

4	large potatoes	4
2 oz.	extra extra old Cheddar cheese, grated	55 g
½ cup	sour cream (regular or low-fat)	125 mL
1 tbsp.	minced green onion	15 mL
¼ cup	milk	60 mL

Preheat oven to 425°F (220°C).

Bake cleaned, unpeeled potatoes for about 40 minutes, until a knife slides in and out easily. Remove from the oven. Reduce the heat to 375°F (190°C).

Cut the potatoes in half lengthwise. (You may want to wear an oven mitt). Gently scoop out the middle and around the sides without tearing the jacket. Whip the scooped-out potato pulp with the rest of the ingredients until fairly smooth. Put the stuffing back into the potato skins. (You can make this ahead to this point, cover and refrigerate, and add an extra 5 minutes baking time.)

Bake at 375°F (190°C) for about 15 minutes, to heat through and melt the cheese.

BAKED CREAMED POTATOES

A partial make-ahead dish.
Serves 6.

A rich mashed potato that you can prepare well in advance.

8	potatoes, peeled	8
4 oz.	cream cheese, softened (regular or low-fat)	115 g
½ cup	sour cream (regular or low-fat)	125 mL
¼ cup	freshly grated Parmesan cheese	60 mL
¼ tsp.	salt	1 mL
¼ tsp.	pepper	1 mL

Boil the potatoes until tender, about 20 minutes. Drain.

Preheat oven to 350°F (180°C).

Mash the potatoes with the rest of the ingredients. Put in a 3-quart (3 L) casserole. (You can make this ahead to this point, cover and refrigerate, and add 5 minutes baking time.)

Bake, uncovered, for about 25 minutes.

ROMANO POTATOES

A partial make-ahead dish.
Serves 6.

Another easy, rich-tasting potato recipe.

8	potatoes, peeled	8
½ cup	freshly grated Romano cheese	125 mL
¼ cup	milk (a little more if necessary)	60 mL
½ tsp.	pepper	2 mL

Boil the potatoes until tender, about 20 minutes. Drain.

Preheat oven to 350°F (180°C).

Mash the potatoes with the rest of the ingredients. Put in a 3-quart (3 L) casserole. (You can make this ahead to this point, cover and refrigerate, and add 5 minutes baking time.)

Bake, uncovered, for 20 minutes.

SCALLOPED POTATOES & BROCCOLI

A partial make-ahead dish.
Serves 4.

This is great when you want everything prepared ahead of time, because it combines two vegetables in a great-tasting casserole.

2 tbsp.	butter	30 mL
2 tbsp.	flour	30 mL
1½ cups	milk	375 mL
2 tbsp.	sherry	30 mL
1 cup	grated sharp Cheddar cheese	250 mL
¼ tsp.	salt	1 mL
¼ tsp.	pepper	1 mL
4	medium potatoes, thinly sliced	4
2 cups	small broccoli florets	500 mL

Preheat oven to 350°F (180°C).

Melt the butter over medium heat. Add the flour and stir about 1 minute. Very slowly add the milk, stirring constantly until smooth. Add the sherry, cheese, salt and pepper, and stir until well-mixed. Turn off the heat and let sit while you're getting the vegetables ready. It will thicken slightly as it sits on the stove.

Spread ¼ cup (60 mL) sauce over the bottom of an 8" (20 cm) square greased casserole. Put half of the potatoes on the bottom, then all of the broccoli, half of the remaining sauce, the rest of the potatoes and the rest of the sauce. (You can make this ahead to this point, cover and refrigerate, and add an extra 10 minutes baking time.)

Bake, covered, for 45 minutes. Remove cover and cook 15 minutes.

HOT POTATO SALAD

A partial make-ahead dish.
Serves 10.

If you are serving this with a highly seasoned dish such as sauerbraten, use white wine; with a less spicy meat, use white wine vinegar for a more tart flavor.

¼ lb.	lean bacon, chopped, trim off fat, if you wish	115 g
⅓ cup	finely chopped green onion	75 mL
⅓ cup	finely chopped celery	75 mL
⅓ cup	finely chopped green pepper	75 mL
1½ tbsp.	flour	22 mL
1 tsp.	dried basil leaves	5 mL
½ tsp.	dry mustard	2 mL
1 cup	chicken broth	250 mL
½ cup	white wine or white wine vinegar	125 mL
12	potatoes	12

Over medium heat, cook the bacon, onion, celery and green pepper for about 5 minutes, stirring occasionally. Add the flour, basil and dry mustard and stir about 1 minute. Very slowly stir in the chicken broth and wine, stirring constantly until smooth. Simmer about 10 minutes, uncovered. (You can make this ahead to this point, cover and refrigerate, and reheat gently.)

Meanwhile, in a large saucepan, cover the potatoes with water; bring to a boil, and cook for about 20 minutes, until they are just tender.

Drain the potatoes and cut into about 1" (2.5 cm) cubes. Pour the hot dressing over the potatoes and mix gently but well.

POTATO PIE
A partial make-ahead dish.
Serves 6.

A tasty way to serve potatoes. These wedges add a little character to the plate.

6	medium potatoes	6
½ cup	sour cream (regular or low-fat)	125 mL
¼ cup	milk	60 mL
2 tbsp.	grated onion	30 mL
¼ tsp.	salt	1 mL
¼ tsp.	pepper	1 mL
1 tbsp.	olive oil	15 mL

In a 3-quart (3 L) pot, boil peeled potatoes until tender and drain.

Preheat oven to 350°F (180°C).

Mash the potatoes with sour cream, milk, onion, salt and pepper. Spread into a well-greased 9" (23 cm) pie plate. Brush the top with olive oil. (You can make this ahead to this point, cover and refrigerate, and add an extra 5 minutes baking time.)

Bake for 20 minutes. Turn oven to broil and cook for 2-3 minutes until lightly browned. Serve in wedges, removing carefully.

SAFFRON RICE
Serves 6-8.

Just a tiny pinch of saffron gives a whole new look and taste.

1/2-2 tbsp.	olive oil	7-30 mL
2	garlic cloves, crushed	2
1/3 cup	minced red onion	75 mL
2 cups	long-grain rice	500 mL
1/4 tsp.	crumbled saffron	1 mL
2 cups	water	500 mL
2 cups	chicken broth	500 mL

In a 3-quart (3 L) pot, heat the oil over medium-high heat, add the garlic and onion and cook for about 2 minutes. Add rice and stir and cook for 3-5 minutes until nicely browned. Stir in saffron; add water and broth. Bring to low simmer. Cover and cook for about 20 minutes, until all the liquid is absorbed.

PEPPER RICE
Serves 4.

This is a very pretty and tasty rice dish.

1/2-1 tbsp.	olive oil	7-15 mL
2	garlic cloves, crushed	2
1/2	green pepper, finely chopped	1/2
1/2	sweet red pepper, finely chopped	1/2
1 cup	long-grain rice	250 mL
2 cups	chicken broth	500 mL

In a 2-quart (2 L) pot, heat the oil over medium-high heat. Add the garlic and green and red peppers and cook for about 3 minutes, stirring often. Add the rice and stir for about 3 minutes, until starting to brown slightly. Add the broth, stir well, and bring to a low simmer. Reduce heat to low, cover and cook for about 20 minutes, until all the liquid is absorbed.

BAKED ITALIAN RICE
Serves 6-8.

Rice with a rich, warm, Italian taste.

1/2-2 tbsp.	olive oil	7-30 mL
4	garlic cloves, crushed	4
2 tsp.	dried basil	10 mL
2	tomatoes, chopped	2
2 cups	long-grain rice	500 mL
4 cups	chicken broth	1 L

Preheat oven to 350°F (180°C).

In a 3-quart (3 L) pot, heat the oil over medium-high heat; add the garlic, basil and tomatoes and cook for about 3 minutes, stirring often. Add the rice and stir for about 2 minutes. Add the broth and stir well.

Cover and bring to a boil. Immediately remove to the oven and bake for about 25 minutes, until all the liquid is absorbed.

RICE WITH ALMONDS & CELERY
Serves 6-8.

A simple rice dish with a nutty flavor and texture.

1/2-2 tbsp.	olive oil	7-30 mL
1/4 cup	minced almonds	60 mL
2/3 cup	minced celery	150 mL
2 cups	long-grain rice	500 mL
4 cups	water	1 L

In a 3-quart (3 L) pot, heat the oil over medium-high heat; add the almonds and celery and cook about 2 minutes. Add the rice and stir and cook for about 2 minutes. Add the water, bring to a simmer, reduce the heat to low. Cover and cook for about 20 minutes, until all the liquid is absorbed.

RICE CONQUISTO

A partial make-ahead dish.
Serves 6.

Plan to have leftover rice so that you can make this moist and delicious casserole. Great as a Mexican side dish. The ingredients are also flexible — use different cheeses, or different vegetables, or green olives instead of black.

2 tbsp.	olive oil	30 mL
3	garlic cloves, crushed	3
1	onion, chopped	1
1 cup	sliced mushrooms	250 mL
1/2 tsp.	chili powder	2 mL
4 cups	cooked rice	1 L
2/3 cup	sliced black olives	150 mL
1/2 cup	grated feta cheese	125 mL
1 1/2 cups	grated Cheddar cheese	375 mL

Preheat oven to 350°F (180°C).

In a 2-quart (2 L) pot, heat the oil over medium-high heat, add the garlic, onion, mushrooms and chili powder. Cook for about 5 minutes, until the onion is slightly soft. Add the rice; stir and cook about 3 minutes.

Stir in the olives and put in a 3-quart (3 L) casserole. Top with the feta and then cheddar. (You can make ahead to this point, cover and refrigerate, and add 5 minutes baking time.)

Bake, uncovered, for 25 minutes.

Note: To pit black olives, press gently on the olive with the flat of a knife blade. The stone will detach from the olive more easily.

CURRIED RICE
Serves 6-8.

Very flavorful and aromatic, with a slightly crunchy texture.

2 tbsp.	olive oil	30 mL
2	garlic cloves, crushed	2
1 tsp.	cinnamon	5 mL
1 tsp.	coriander	5 mL
1 tsp.	cumin	5 mL
2 cups	long-grain rice (preferably Basmati)	500 mL
4 cups	water	1 L

In a 3-quart (3 L) pot, heat the oil over medium-high heat. Add the garlic, spices and rice and cook, stirring constantly, for about 5 minutes. Add the water and bring to simmer. Cover and cook for about 20 minutes, until all the liquid is absorbed.

Note: Most Indian cooks make their own curry powder fresh each day, blending up to 20 herbs, spices and seeds. Commercial curry powder is not the same but, if you wish, substitute 2 tsp. (10 mL) of curry powder for the cinnamon, coriander and cumin.

See photograph on page 137.

Keep seldom-used spices in the refrigerator so they will retain their freshness longer.

INDONESIAN RICE

Serves 6-8.

The coconut milk gives this dish an added richness.

2 tbsp.	olive oil	30 mL
2	garlic cloves, crushed	2
1 tsp.	curry powder	5 mL
2	1" (2.5 cm) dried red chili peppers	2
2 cups	long-grain rice (preferably Basmati)	500 mL
14 oz.	can coconut milk (light or regular)	398 mL
2½ cups	water	625 mL

In a 3-quart (3 L) pot, heat the oil over medium-high heat, add the garlic, curry, chili peppers and rice. Stir and cook for about 3 minutes. Add the coconut milk and water. Bring to a simmer, reduce the heat to low and cook for about 20 minutes, until all the liquid is absorbed. Remove chili peppers before serving.

Note: Basmati rice grows in India. It has a lovely, distinctive aroma and a nut-like flavor. It is a long-grained, fine-textured rice.

Unless otherwise stated, all rice recipes in this book use 20-minute long-grain rice, not precooked or quick rice.

PASTA

PASTAS, SEAFOODS & MEATS

ORIENTAL VEGETABLES & VERMICELLI

Serves 6 as a side dish; 3-4 as a light lunch.

Crunchy vegetables and skinny noodles make a wonderful combination, and you won't need to make anything else besides this to go with the main course.

4 oz.	rice vermicelli or rice stick (approximately)	115 g
1-2 tbsp.	oil	15-30 mL
2 tbsp.	minced ginger	30 mL
3	cloves garlic, crushed	3
3	1" (2.5 cm) dried red chili peppers	3
1 tbsp.	dark soy sauce	15 mL
3 cups	vegetables (small broccoli florets, 1/4" (1 cm) slices celery, 1/2" (1.3 cm) pieces green and sweet red pepper, halved mushrooms, thinly sliced onion, etc.)	750 mL
1 1/2 cups	chicken broth	375 mL
2 tbsp.	cornstarch	30 mL
3 tbsp.	water	45 mL

Cover the vermicelli with boiling water, cover and set aside for 10-15 minutes, until tender.

Meanwhile, in a large frying pan over high heat, cook the oil, ginger, garlic, chili peppers, soy sauce, and vegetables, stirring almost constantly, for about 5 minutes. Add the chicken broth and bring to a medium boil.

Mix the cornstarch and water and stir this into the broth. Reduce heat to low-medium, so the liquid is just simmering. Cover and simmer for 3 minutes. Drain the vermicelli and put in a shallow dish. Pour the sauce and vegetables evenly over the noodles. Remove chili peppers before serving.

See photograph on page 155.

In many recipes, including many in this book, you can decrease the oil required in frying meat and vegetables simply by using a nonstick pan.

CHEESY HERB FETTUCCINE
With snow peas & red pepper.
A partial make-ahead dish.
Serves 6-8 as a side dish, 3-4 as a light lunch.

So rich, so tasty and so pretty.

12 oz.	fettuccine (or similar pasta)	340 g
1 tbsp.	olive oil	15 mL
2	garlic cloves, crushed	2
1 tsp.	dried basil	5 mL
1 tsp.	dried oregano leaves	5 mL
2	1" (2.5 cm) dried red chili peppers	2
1 cup	chicken broth	250 mL
1/3 cup	white wine	75 mL
36	small snow peas, trimmed	36
1	sweet red pepper, slivered	1
1/2 cup	freshly grated Parmesan cheese	125 mL
1/2 cup	grated feta cheese	125 mL

Boil the fettuccine until barely tender. Drain and rinse with hot water.

Meanwhile, in a 1-quart (1 L) pot over medium-high heat, cook the oil, garlic, basil, oregano and chilies for about 3 minutes. Add the chicken broth and wine, bring to low boil and cook for about 3 minutes.

In a 3-quart (3 L) casserole, toss the seasoned broth with the noodles, snow peas, sweet red pepper and cheeses. (If you are making this ahead, rinse the noodles again in cold water and chill the broth before combining. Then cover and refrigerate, and add 5 minutes baking time.)

Bake, covered, at 350°F (180°C) for about 25 minutes. Remove the cover, stir and bake for about another 10 minutes, until the cheese is completely melted. Remove chili peppers before serving.

See photograph on page 173.

PERFECT PESTO
A partial make-ahead dish.
Serves 12.

Originally Pesto was made in Genoa, Italy. It makes a wonderfully simple and delicious pasta topping and can also be used to enhance chicken and fish dishes.

2 cups	fresh basil leaves (about 2 oz. [55 g])	500 mL
¾ cup	pine nuts, (see note page 24)	175 mL
1½ cups	freshly grated Parmesan cheese	375 mL
4 tsp.	freshly crushed garlic (about 6 cloves)	20 mL
1 tsp.	freshly grated black pepper	5 mL
1 tsp.	salt	5 mL
½ cup	extra virgin olive oil	125 mL

Put basil, pine nuts, Parmesan, garlic, pepper and salt into the food processor and process until evenly grainy. With the machine still running, slowly pour in the olive oil and continue to process until smooth, about 1 minute in total.

Distribute Pesto evenly in an ice cube tray (12 cubes, about 2 tbsp. [30 mL] each). Cover with waxed paper and freeze for about 6 hours. Transfer cubes to a freezer bag and keep frozen until ready to use.

To Serve: For 4 servings, completely thaw 4 cubes of pesto. Cook 1½ lbs. (1 kg) of spaghetti or other pasta. Drain well. Meanwhile, just before spaghetti is ready, boil ⅔ cup (150 mL) chicken broth in a small pot. Quickly whisk in the Pesto cubes. Immediately drain spaghetti and toss with the Pesto mixture. Serve and season with salt, pepper and freshly grated Parmesan or Romano cheese.

For pasta casseroles that you want to bake later, be sure the pasta and the sauce have cooled before combining them in the casserole. If they're both really hot, the dish tends to end up gummy and overcooked.

106

ORZO WITH SWEET TOMATO WINE SAUCE

A partial make-ahead dish.
Serves 6 as a side dish.

If you can't decide between pasta or rice, try orzo. This rice-sized pasta tastes great with a slightly sweet aromatic sauce drizzled over top.

1-2 tbsp.	extra virgin olive oil	15-30 mL
2	garlic cloves, crushed	2
2 tsp.	dried oregano	10 mL
6	Roma or Italian plum tomatoes, chopped, or other tomatoes	6
2 tbsp.	sugar	30 mL
¼ cup	white wine	60 mL
12 oz.	orzo pasta	340 g

Heat the oil over medium heat, add the garlic and oregano and cook for about 1 minute. Add the tomatoes, sugar and wine and stir well. Bring to a gentle simmer. Cover and cook about 15 minutes. (You can make this ahead to this point, cover and refrigerate; reheat gently.)

Meanwhile, boil the orzo until tender. Drain the orzo, put on plates and drizzle the sauce over the top.

CREAMY VEGETABLE FUSILLI

Serves 6 as a side dish.

A colorful, tangy side dish that goes well with a plain main course.

12 oz.	vegetable fusilli or similar pasta	340 g
4 oz.	cream cheese (regular or low-fat)	115 g
⅔ cup	yogurt (regular or low-fat)	150 mL
½ tsp.	dried dill	2 mL

Cook the fusilli until tender.

Meanwhile, in a 1-quart (1 L) pot, melt the cream cheese over low heat. Add the yogurt and dill and heat through. Stir well.

Drain the pasta and toss with the hot creamy dressing.

SIMPLE SIDE SHELLS
A partial make-ahead dish.
Serves 6 as a side dish.

This is a very simple side dish for when you need something tasty but not exotic.

12 oz.	small shell or similar pasta	340 g
1-2 tbsp.	olive oil	15-30 mL
1 cup	hot chicken broth	250 mL
1 tsp.	Worcestershire sauce	5 mL
½ cup	frozen peas, rinsed under hot water and drained	125 mL

Preheat oven to 325°F (160°C).

Boil the shells until just barely tender. Drain, rinse with hot water. Toss with the rest of the ingredients, and put in a 3-quart (3 L) casserole. (If you are making this ahead, rinse the shells again with cold water and chill the broth before combining. Then, cover and refrigerate, and add 5 minutes baking time.)

Bake, covered, for about 15 minutes. Remove cover, stir, and bake for about 5 minutes. Stir again and serve.

SAUCE FRANÇAISE À LA TOMATE
A partial make-ahead dish.
Serves 4.

For flavour and simplicity, this is a fabulous sauce, but you must use fresh basil, not dried.

3 tbsp.	extra-virgin olive oil	45 mL
2	garlic cloves, crushed	2
1	small onion, chopped	1
19 oz.	can tomatoes, chopped	540 mL
¼ tsp.	salt	1 mL
¼ tsp.	pepper	1 mL
¼ cup	chopped fresh basil (must be fresh!)	60 mL
1-1½ lbs.	fettuccine or similar pasta	500-750 g

In a 2-quart (2 L) pot, heat the oil over medium heat; add the garlic and onion and cook for 5 minutes, until onion is slightly soft, stirring often. Add the tomatoes, salt and pepper and cook for 5 minutes. Add the basil and continue cooking for about 15 minutes, stirring often, until sauce is thick and rich. (You can make this ahead to this point, cover, and reheat gently.)

Meanwhile, cook the fettuccine just until tender. Drain, toss well with the sauce, and serve.

PASTA WITH SUN-DRIED TOMATOES
A partial make-ahead dish.
Serves 4 as a main dish.

This is such a pleasing, pretty and satisfying dish, it will leave you wanting more.

2-4 tbsp.	extra virgin olive oil	30-60 mL
3	garlic cloves, crushed	3
1/4 cup	chopped fresh basil	60 mL
2	1" (2.5 cm) dried red chili peppers	2
1	sweet red pepper, cut into matchstick size	1
1/2 tsp.	pepper	2 mL
1 tsp.	salt	5 mL
1 1/2 oz.	(dry weight) sun-dried tomatoes	42 g
3/4 cup	chicken broth	175 mL
1/4 cup	white wine	60 mL
1-1 1/2 lbs.	fettuccine or similar pasta	500-750 g

Put the oil, garlic, basil, dried red chilies, red pepper, pepper, salt and sun-dried tomatoes in a 2-quart (2 L) pot and bring to a light sizzle over medium-high heat. Cook for about 5 minutes, stirring occasionally. Add the chicken broth and wine, reduce heat and simmer gently for about 15 minutes, uncovered. (You can make this ahead to this point, cover and refrigerate, and reheat gently.)

Meanwhile, boil the fettuccine until just tender. Drain the pasta and toss it with the sauce. Remove chili peppers before serving.

These may be messy to make, but once stuffed, the whole meal is ready.

FETA-STUFFED CANNELLONI

A partial make-ahead dish.
Serves 6.

2-3 tbsp.	olive oil	30-45 mL
1 tsp.	dried oregano	5 mL
1/2	onion, finely chopped	1/2
19 oz.	can tomatoes, chopped	540 mL
14 oz.	can crushed tomatoes	398 mL
14 oz.	can tomato sauce	398 mL
1/2 cup	red wine	125 mL
2 tbsp.	sugar	30 mL
10 oz.	feta cheese, crumbled	285 g
10 oz.	pkg. frozen chopped spinach, thawed and drained	283 g
2	garlic cloves, crushed	2
2	eggs, beaten	2
1 tsp.	dill	5 mL
1	large tomato, finely chopped	1
7 oz.	pkg. oven-ready cannelloni (about 20 tubes)	200 g
1/4 cup	freshly grated Parmesan cheese	60 mL

In a 3-quart (3 L) pot, heat the oil over medium heat; add the oregano and onion and cook for about 5 minutes, stirring frequently. Add the tomatoes, crushed tomatoes, tomato sauce, wine and sugar. Stir well and simmer for about 30 minutes.

Preheat oven to 350°F (180°C).

Mix the feta, spinach, garlic, eggs, dill and tomato. Lightly fill the cannelloni tubes, pushing down with a spoon into one end, while closing off the other end with the palm of your hand.

Put about 1½ cups (375 mL) tomato sauce in the bottom of a 9 x 13" (22 x 33 cm) pan and spread evenly. Place stuffed cannelloni on top of the sauce in a single layer, spacing evenly in the pan. Pour the rest of the sauce over to cover all the tubes. (If you want to make this ahead, be sure the sauce is cold before assembling the dish, cover and refrigerate, and add an extra 10 minutes to the baking time.) Cover and bake for 45 minutes. Remove the cover; sprinkle with Parmesan and bake 10 minutes. Let sit for about 5 minutes before serving.

FETA FETTUCCINE WITH ARTICHOKES

A partial make-ahead dish.
Serves 4.

A wonderful combination of flavors, tangy feta, herbs and artichokes in a spicy tomato, garlic sauce.

1-2 tbsp.	oil	15-30 mL
1/2	onion, finely chopped	1/2
2	garlic cloves, crushed	2
2 tbsp.	dried basil	30 mL
1 tsp.	dried oregano leaves	5 mL
1 tsp.	dried tarragon	5 mL
1	1" (2.5 cm) dried red chili pepper (crushed if you like it hot)	1
19 oz.	can tomatoes, chopped	540 mL
7 1/2 oz.	can tomato sauce	213 mL
5 1/2 oz.	can tomato paste	156 mL
1/3 cup	red wine	75 mL
14 oz.	can artichokes, drained, coarsely chopped	398 mL
6 oz.	feta cheese, in 1/3" (8 mm) cubes	170 g
1/3 cup	sliced black olives	75 mL
1-1 1/2 lbs.	fettuccine	500-750 g
	Parmesan or Romano cheese	

In a 3-quart (3 L) pot, heat the oil over medium heat. Add the onion, garlic, basil, oregano, tarragon and chili pepper. Cook, stirring frequently, about 5 minutes. Add the tomatoes, tomato sauce, tomato paste and wine. Simmer gently for about 30 minutes, uncovered. (You can make this ahead to this point, cover and refrigerate, and reheat gently.)

Add the artichokes, feta and olives. Let sit on very low heat until heated through and the feta has softened but not melted.

Meanwhile, cook the fettuccine until just tender. Serve the sauce over the drained noodles and pass some freshly grated Parmesan or Romano cheese, if desired. Remove whole chili pepper before serving.

FOUR CHEESE ROTINI

A partial make-ahead dish.
Serves 4.

Also known as Gourmet Macaroni and Cheese! This is very tasty and rich, with a wonderful mixture of cheeses, especially the Asiago.

1 lb.	rotini or similar pasta	500 g
2 tbsp.	butter	30 mL
2 tbsp.	flour	30 mL
2 cups	milk	500 mL
2/3 cup	grated Asiago cheese	150 mL
2/3 cup	grated extra extra old or sharp Cheddar cheese	150 mL
1 cup	grated mozzarella	250 mL
1/4 tsp.	cayenne pepper	1 mL
1/3 cup	white wine	75 mL
1/4 cup	freshly grated Romano cheese	60 mL
1/4 cup	fine bread crumbs	60 mL

Preheat oven to 350°F (180°C).

Boil the rotini until just barely tender. Drain and rinse with hot water.

Meanwhile, melt the butter over medium heat; add the flour and stir for about 1 minute. Slowly add the milk, stirring constantly for about 5 minutes. Stir in the Asiago, Cheddar and mozzarella. Turn off the heat. Stir in the cayenne pepper and the wine.

Combine the sauce and pasta in a pot and mix gently but well. Pour into a 9 x 13" (23 x 33 cm) casserole. Mix the Romano cheese and bread crumbs and sprinkle over the top. Cover closely. (You can make this ahead to this point, but rinse the rotini again in cold water, and let the sauce cool to room temperature before combining. Then cover and refrigerate and add an extra 5 minutes baking time.)

Cover and bake for 20 minutes. Remove the cover and continue baking for about 5 minutes, until bubbling around the edges.

SPAGHETTI ESPANOLE

A partial make-ahead dish.
Serves 6.

So good, so easy — spaghetti sauce with a difference. Notice there are no added herbs or spices — the flavor comes straight from the main ingredients.

1 tbsp.	olive oil	15 mL
¼ lb.	bacon, fat trimmed, chopped	115 g
1 lb.	raw spicy sausage, e.g. chorizo, in ½" (1.3 cm) slices	500 g
1	small onion, chopped	1
2	green peppers, chopped	2
1	large sweet red pepper, chopped	1
19 oz.	can tomatoes, chopped	540 mL
7½ oz.	can tomato sauce	213 mL
5½ oz.	can tomato paste	156 mL
½ tbsp.	pickled capers, with juice	7 mL
¼cup	red wine	60 mL
¼ cup	halved green olives	60 mL
2 lbs.	spaghetti	1 kg

In a 3-quart (3 L) pot, heat the oil over medium-high heat. Add the bacon, sausage, onion, green pepper and red pepper, and cook about 10 minutes, stirring frequently. Drain off the excess fat, if desired.

Add the rest of the ingredients and stir well. Bring to a simmer. Reduce heat to low. Cover and cook for about 2 hours, or more, stirring occasionally. (This can be made ahead, covered and refrigerated, and reheated gently.)

Meanwhile, cook the spaghetti just until tender. Serve the sauce over the drained noodles.

See photograph on page 101.

When something must first come to a boil and then gently simmer, and the burner that it is on is retaining too much heat, have another burner turned to low heat and transfer the pot there once it has reached the boiling point.

SPAGHETTI SAUCE
A make-ahead dish.
Makes enough sauce for 12 servings.

Don't bother to halve this recipe for a smaller group. It freezes well and can be used in a variety of ways (see below).

3 lbs.	ground beef	
1½ cups	finely chopped green pepper	375 mL
1½ cups	finely chopped celery	375 mL
1½ cups	finely chopped onion	375 mL
4	garlic cloves, crushed	4
28 oz.	can tomatoes, chopped	796 mL
28 oz.	can tomato sauce	796 mL
13 oz.	can tomato paste	369 mL
1 tbsp.	dried oregano	15 mL
1 tbsp.	dried basil leaves	15 mL
1½ tsp.	dried tarragon leaves	7 mL
½ tsp.	cayenne	2 mL
2	bay leaves	2
1 cup	water	250 mL
¾ cup	red wine	175 mL

In a large pot or Dutch oven, cook the ground beef over medium-high heat until no longer pink, about 20 minutes, stirring often. Drain off the excess fat in a colander (rinse with hot water if you want to get rid of even more fat) and return to the pot.

Add the green pepper, celery, onion and garlic and cook for about 5 minutes, stirring often. Add the rest of the ingredients, stir well and cook over low heat for 2-4 hours, uncovered, stirring often. Remove bay leaves before serving. (You can make this ahead to this point, cover and refrigerate, and reheat gently.)

Serve over spaghetti (1 lb. [500 g] for 3-4 people).

Variations: QUICK CHILI: Using about ⅓ of this recipe, add 1 tbsp. chili powder and 2, 14 oz. (2, 398 mL) cans kidney beans, drained. Cook over low-medium heat for about 30 minutes. Serves 4 like this, or more if you serve it over rice.

SPAGHETTI SAUCE
Continued

NACHO DIP: *Using about 2 cups (500 mL) spaghetti sauce, add ¼ cup (60 mL) minced jalapeño peppers and cook over low-medium heat for about 15 minutes. Use as a dip for nacho chips, along with some sour cream or yogurt.*

ADD TO SOUP: *If you want to add some zest to turkey soup, add 1-2 cups (250-500 mL) spaghetti sauce to a pot of soup for a livelier taste.*

SLOPPY SLOPPY JOES: *Pour about 1 cup (250 mL) of hot spaghetti sauce over 1 or 2 thick slices of bread or bun halves. (You'll need a knife and fork for this sandwich.) Sprinkle with Parmesan cheese, if you like.*

LINGUINE & RED CLAM SAUCE
A partial make-ahead dish.
Serves 4.

Simple and delicious.

2-4 tbsp.	butter	30-60 mL
4	garlic cloves, crushed	4
1 tsp.	dried oregano leaves	5 mL
⅓ cup	chopped fresh basil (or 2 tsp. [10 mL] dried)	75 mL
½ tsp.	pepper	2 mL
⅓ cup	red wine	75 mL
19 oz.	can tomatoes, chopped	540 mL
2 x 5 oz.	cans clams (do not drain)	2 x 142 g
1-1½ lbs.	linguine (or similar pasta)	500-750 g

In a 2-quart (2 L) pot, melt the butter over medium heat. Add the garlic, oregano, basil and pepper. Stir and cook about 2 minutes. Add the wine, tomatoes and clams with their juice. Bring to a simmer and cook about 15 minutes. (You can make this ahead to this point, cover and refrigerate, and reheat gently.)

Meanwhile, cook the linguine until just tender. Toss the drained noodles with the sauce and serve with freshly grated Parmesan or Romano cheese, if desired.

SEAFOOD LASAGNE

A partial make-ahead dish.
Serves 6-8.

This has a light white sauce that's not too rich, thanks to using chicken broth instead of more cream. Also try different seafood combinations.

¼ cup	butter	60 mL
3	garlic cloves, crushed	3
½ cup	finely minced red onion	125 mL
1 cup	thinly sliced mushrooms	250 mL
2 tsp.	curry powder	10 mL
3 tbsp.	flour	45 mL
2 cups	chicken broth	500 mL
1 cup	milk	250 mL
1 cup	35% cream (whipping cream)	250 mL
½ cup	white wine	125 mL
12-15	oven-ready lasagne noodles	12-15
½ lb.	raw salad shrimp (or large shrimp, chopped)	250 g
½ lb.	large raw scallops, quartered	250 g
2 x 4 oz.	cans crab, drained	2 x 115 g
¼ cup	freshly grated Parmesan cheese	60 mL
1 cup	grated mozzarella cheese	250 mL

Preheat oven to 350°F (180°C).

In a 2-quart (2 L) pot, melt the butter over medium heat. Add the garlic, onion, mushrooms and curry powder. Cook about 6 minutes, stirring frequently, until the mushrooms have softened. Add the flour and stir about 1 minute to make a paste. Very slowly, add the chicken broth, stirring constantly, until smooth. (Using a whisk will make this easier.) Slowly stir in the milk, then cream, then wine. Let simmer gently for about 15 minutes, stirring occasionally.

In the bottom of a 9 x 13" (23 x 33 cm) pan, spread 1 cup (250 mL) of the sauce. Lay 4-5 lasagne noodles in a single layer on top of the sauce. Top with chopped shrimp and scallops, then about 1 cup (250 mL) of the sauce spread evenly over the seafood. Layer on another 4-5 noodles, then crabmeat and Parmesan, then about 1 cup (250 mL) of sauce, another 4 to 5 noodles, the rest of the sauce, and top with mozzarella. (If you want to make this ahead, be sure that the cream sauce has cooled completely before assembling the lasagne, cover and refrigerate; add about 5 minutes, covered, baking time.)

SEAFOOD LASAGNE
Continued

Cover tightly with foil and bake for about 40 minutes. Remove the cover, increase oven temperature to broil, and broil for about 3 minutes, until the cheese is just lightly browned. Remove from the oven and let sit for about 5 minutes before serving.

To Serve: *Serve with French bread and a colorful salad, such as Parsley and Tomato, page 74, or Greek Salad, page 67.*

PASTA SHELLS & BROCCOLI CLAM SAUCE
Serves 4.

A quick, easy versatile meal. Try substituting other vegetables for the broccoli.

1-2 tbsp.	olive oil	15-30 mL
4	garlic cloves, crushed	
2 tsp.	dried basil	10 mL
1 tsp.	dried oregano	5 mL
¼ tsp.	pepper	1 mL
1	onion, finely chopped	1
3 cups	small broccoli florets	750 mL
2 x 5 oz.	cans baby clams (do not drain)	2 x 142 g
1 cup	white wine	250 mL
1-1¼ lbs.	small shell or similar pasta	500-615 g

In a 2-quart (2 L) pot, heat oil over medium-high heat. Add garlic, basil, oregano, pepper and onion; cook, stirring frequently, about 5 minutes. Stir in the broccoli, clams, clam juice and wine. Bring to a low boil and simmer, uncovered, about 10 minutes; stir occasionally.

Meanwhile, cook the shells until just tender.

Toss the drained shells with the sauce and serve, being careful to give each serving its share of the clams and broccoli. Serve with freshly grated Parmesan or Romano cheese, if desired.

SHRIMP & PEPPERS

Serves 4.

Here is a quick and easy complete supper, for one of those nights when you're tired after a long winter's day.

1-2 tbsp.	olive oil	15-30 mL
2	garlic cloves, crushed	2
4	1" (2.5 cm) dried red chili peppers	4
1	large green pepper, chopped	1
1	large sweet red pepper, chopped	1
¼ cup	chopped cilantro (optional)	60 mL
1 lb.	large shrimp, peeled	500 g
2 cups	hot chicken broth	500 mL
1 lb.	vermicelli noodles or similar pasta	500 g

In a large frying pan, heat the oil over medium-high heat. Add the garlic, chili peppers, green and red peppers and cook and stir about 5 minutes.

Turn the heat to high; add the cilantro and shrimp and stir for 30 seconds. Add the chicken broth. As soon as this comes to a boil, remove it from the heat, cover and set aside for about 3 minutes. Remove chili peppers before serving.

Meanwhile, cook the vermicelli just until tender. Serve the noodles in a shallow bowl and top with the shrimp mixture.

To Serve: Serve with lots of French bread.

SEAFOOD

Citrus Grilled Shrimp, page 122
Pasta Vegetable Salad, page 71
Cheese Biscuits, page 54

SHRIMP & SUN-DRIED TOMATOES

A partial make-ahead dish.
Serves 4.

A rich-tasting combination of flavors that leaves you feeling pampered.

1 tbsp.	olive oil	15 mL
½ cup	minced green onions, bottoms only	125 mL
1	large green pepper, thinly sliced	1
1 tbsp.	flour	15 mL
¾ cup	chicken broth	175 mL
¼ cup	vermouth	60 mL
⅓ cup	chopped fresh cilantro	75 mL
1½ oz.	(dry weight) sun-dried tomatoes, chopped	42 g
½ tsp.	salt	2 mL
¼ tsp.	pepper	1 mL
⅓ cup	35% cream (whipping cream)	75 mL
1 lb.	large raw shrimp, peeled and deveined	500 g

In a 2-quart (2 L) pot, heat the oil over medium heat, add the onion and green pepper and cook for 5 minutes, stirring often.

Stir in the flour for about 1 minute. Slowly stir in the chicken broth and vermouth, stirring constantly until smooth. Stir in the cilantro and sun-dried tomatoes. Bring to a low boil and simmer, uncovered, for about 5 minutes. (You can make this ahead to this point, cover and refrigerate, and reheat gently.)

Stir in the salt, pepper and cream. Increase the heat to high and bring to a boil. Add the shrimp, cover and cook for 2-3 minutes, just until shrimp are pink.

To Serve: Serve over 1 lb. (500 g) linguini or 12 oz. (340 g) broad egg noodles.

GARLIC SHRIMP
Serves 4.

When you really want to treat yourself, try this buttery garlicky concoction. It's ready in no time, but you have to cook the shrimp at the last minute. Provide lots of napkins because peeling shrimp is a messy business.

¼ cup	butter	60 mL
1 tbsp.	lemon juice	15 mL
¼ cup	chicken broth	60 mL
4	garlic cloves, crushed	4
⅛-¼ tsp.	Tabasco sauce	0.5-2 mL
1 lb.	shrimp, shells on, rinsed	500 g

In a large frying pan, over high heat, cook the butter, lemon juice, broth, garlic and Tabasco until boiling. Add the shrimp; cook and stir just until all the shrimp are pink, about 2-3 minutes.

To Serve: Serve with Light and Zesty Pasta Salad, page 72. If you like the shells, eat them (sounds strange, but some people do, including me!). Otherwise, peel shrimp and discard shells. Soak up the juices with some French bread.

CITRUS GRILLED SHRIMP
Marinating time required.
Serves 4.

Very simple, but be careful not to overcook.

1-2	oranges, juice of (½ cup [125 mL] juice)	1-2
1	lime, juice of (1 tbsp. [15 mL] juice)	1
1 tsp.	bouquet garni (see note on page 53)	5 mL
1 tbsp.	olive oil	15 mL
¼ tsp.	pepper	1 mL
1 lb.	large raw shrimp, peeled and deveined	500 g

CITRUS GRILLED SHRIMP
Continued

In a glass bowl, combine all ingredients, except the shrimp; mix well. Stir in the shrimp. Cover and refrigerate for 8 hours, turning occasionally.

Preheat the barbecue to high heat.

Drain the shrimp. Put on 8 skewers. Barbecue over high heat for 1-2 minutes per side, until all the shrimp are bright pink. Do not overcook. Serve with Rice Conquisto, page 98, and sliced oranges.

See photograph page 119.

See photograph page 119.

FETA AND SHRIMP
A partial make-ahead dish.
Serves 4.

A wonderful combination of flavors, but don't overcook the shrimp.

2 tbsp.	olive oil	30 mL
3	garlic cloves, crushed	3
1	onion, thinly sliced	1
1	large green pepper, in 1" (2.5 cm) chunks	1
12	mushrooms, halved	12
1 tsp.	dried oregano leaves	5 mL
1/4 tsp.	crumbled saffron (optional)	1 mL
2 tsp.	dried basil	10 mL
1/2 tsp.	pepper	2 mL
19 oz.	can tomatoes, chopped	540 mL
1/3 cup	white wine	75 mL
1 lb.	raw large shrimp, shelled	500 g
4 oz.	feta cheese, crumbled	115 g

In a large frying pan, over medium heat, sauté the first 9 ingredients about 10 minutes, stirring occasionally. Add the tomatoes and wine and simmer gently, uncovered, about 20 minutes. (You can make this ahead to this point, cover and refrigerate, and reheat gently.)

Increase heat to medium high, bring to a boil and stir in the shrimp. Cover and cook 2 minutes. Sprinkle with feta; cover; cook until shrimp are pink and the feta barely melted, 1-2 minutes. Serve over rice or pasta, or with French bread to soak up the juices.

SHRIMP & GOUDA QUICHE

A make-ahead dish.
Serves 6-8.

This is a very pretty and tasty quiche. If you're in a hurry, use a commercial unbaked pie shell. For variation, try different types of Gouda, for example spiced Gouda or peppered Gouda. It's really very gooda!

2	unbaked 9" (23 cm) pie shells (see note)	2
10 oz.	cooked shrimp meat (preferably fresh)	285 g
2 cups	grated Gouda cheese	599 mL
3	eggs, beaten	3
1 cup	milk (use half 35% cream for a richer filling)	250 mL
1/2 tsp.	pepper (if using plain Gouda)	2 mL
1/2 cup	finely diced sweet red pepper	125 mL

Preheat oven to 350°F (180°C).

Sprinkle the shrimp over the bottom of the pie shells. Top with cheese. Mix the eggs, milk and pepper and pour over the cheese. Sprinkle the diced red pepper over top. Bake for 25-30 minutes, until barely set. (It will set more as it cools.) Serve hot, warm or cold. (This can be made ahead, covered and refrigerated, and served at the desired temperature.)

To Serve: Serve with a Greek Salad, page 67 or Butter Lettuce Salad, page 58.

Note: There is an excellent pastry recipe included in Apple Date Pie, page 178, or use your own favorite.

PAELLA
A partial make-ahead dish.
Serves 8.

Too pretty to eat. Except for the use of saffron, and the proper ratio of liquid to rice, just about everything in this dish is flexible. Make it to suit your personal taste and budget.

2-4 tbsp.	olive oil	30-60 mL
3	garlic cloves, crushed	3
1	onion, chopped	1
1	green pepper, slivered	1
1 lb.	chicken wings, halved (discard tips)	500 g
1 lb.	raw spicy sausage, in 3/4" (2 cm) slices	500 g
1	sweet red pepper, slivered	1
3 cups	long-grain rice	750 mL
4 cups	chicken broth	1 L
3/4 cup	water	175 mL
1 cup	white wine	250 mL
4	tomatoes, chopped	4
1/4-1/2 tsp.	crumbled saffron	1-2 mL
1/4 tsp.	turmeric	1 mL
1 cup	frozen peas	250 mL
16	fresh mussels, rinsed (be sure all shells are closed, see note, page 31)	16
1 lb.	raw large shrimp, peeled	500 mL
8	lemon wedges	8

In a large wok or Dutch oven, heat the oil over medium-high heat. Add garlic, onion, green pepper, chicken and sausage, and cook 10 minutes, stirring often. Drain off excess fat, if desired. (You can make this ahead to this point, cover, refrigerate and reheat gently.)

Add the red pepper and rice and stir for 1 minute. Add the broth, water, wine, tomatoes, saffron and turmeric. Stir well. Bring to a simmer. Cover and cook for about 15 minutes, until most of the liquid is absorbed but the mixture is not too dry. Stir in the peas. Cover and cook for about 3 minutes.

Place the mussels in the rice (hinged side down, so that mussels will open upwards as they cook), and spread shrimp all around. Cover and cook about 5 minutes, until all the mussels are fully open and the shrimp are pink. Garnish with lemon wedges. Put the cover back on. Bring to the table. Remove cover. Voila!

SHRIMP & SAUSAGE JAMBALAYA

**A partial make-ahead dish.
Serves 6.**

A wonderful spicy one-dish meal. You can also make a Shrimp and Chicken version.

1 lb.	spicy sausage in ½" (1.3 cm) slices	500 g
2	green peppers, diced	2
1	sweet red pepper, diced	1
1	white onion, diced	1
4	garlic cloves, crushed	4
1 tsp.	dried oregano leaves	5 mL
½ tsp.	pepper	2 mL
½ tsp.	cayenne	2 mL
1 tbsp.	dried basil	15 mL
3	jalapeño peppers, seeded and thinly sliced (optional)	3
2	large ripe tomatoes, chopped	2
3 tbsp.	tomato paste	45 mL
1 cup	white wine	250 mL
3 cups	chicken broth	750 mL
2 cups	long-grain rice	500 mL
1 lb.	large raw shrimp, shelled	500 g
¼ cup	slivered fresh cilantro (optional)	60 mL

In a large metal pot (do not use non-stick), cook the sausage over medium-high heat for about 10 minutes, stirring often. Drain off the excess fat.

Add the green pepper, red pepper, onion, garlic, oregano, pepper, cayenne, basil, jalapeño peppers and tomatoes. Stir often, scraping the bottom of the pot, and cook about 10 minutes. (You can make this ahead to this point, cover and refrigerate, and reheat gently.)

Add the tomato paste, wine, broth and rice. Bring to a simmer. Cover and simmer gently for about 20 minutes, until most of the liquid is absorbed.

Stir in the shrimp. Cover and cook until all the shrimp are pink, about 4 minutes. Remove to serving dish and sprinkle with cilantro.

Variation: Add chicken thighs or breasts, boned and cut in bite-sized pieces or substitute them for the sausage. Sauté briefly and proceed as above. Add additional cayenne, if you wish, to compensate for the spice in the sausage.

HALIBUT WITH CAPER SAUCE

A partial make-ahead dish.
Serves 4.

Pretty as well as easy, this fish dish is just delish.

4	halibut steaks (¾-1" [2-2.5 cm] thick)	4
1 tbsp.	melted butter	15 mL
2 tbsp.	butter	30 mL
1 tbsp.	flour	15 mL
¼ tsp.	pepper	1 mL
½ cup	chicken broth	125 mL
¼ cup	35% cream (whipping cream)	60 mL
1 tbsp.	drained capers	15 mL
	lemon wedges	
	fresh parley	

Preheat oven to 450°F (230°C).

Brush the steaks with 1 tbsp. (15 mL) melted butter. Place on a rack over a pan and bake for about 7 minutes, turn and bake another 6 minutes.

Meanwhile, melt 2 tbsp. (30 mL) butter over medium heat, add the flour and pepper and stir for about 1 minute to make a paste. Very slowly add the chicken broth, stirring constantly (preferably with a whisk) until smooth and thickened slightly. Slowly stir in the cream and then the capers. Simmer for about 1 minute. (The sauce only can be made ahead and gently reheated.)

Put 1 tbsp. (15 mL) of sauce on each plate, put the steak on top and pour the rest of the sauce over the steaks.

Garnish with lemon wedges and fresh parsley.

To Serve: Serve with Gingered Broccoli, page 81 and Basil and Tarragon Roasted Potatoes, page 89.

CAJUN SNAPPER
Serves 4.

Cajun heat! You can turn this heat up or down by adding more or less cayenne.

2 lbs.	snapper fillets	1 kg
2 tbsp.	cornmeal	30 mL
1 tsp.	pepper	5 mL
½ tsp.	cayenne	2 mL
1½ tsp.	paprika	7 mL
1 tsp.	dried oregano	5 mL
1 tsp.	chili powder	5 mL
¼ cup	butter (approx.)	60 mL

Cut the fillets to desired size. Mix the cornmeal, pepper, cayenne, paprika, oregano and chili powder. Dip the fillets in the cornmeal mixture, pressing lightly and turning several times.

Heat 1-2 tbsp. (15-30 mL) butter over high heat in a large frying pan. Quickly brown each fillet, turning after 3-5 minutes, depending on the thickness of the fish. Brown the other side for 3-5 minutes. Repeat until all the fish is cooked, keeping cooked fish in a warm oven.

To Serve: Serve with plain rice and Lemony Carrots, page 86.

COD CURRY WITH ALMONDS
Serves 4.

Originally, this Newfoundland recipe adaptation called for a ¹/₂ cup (125 mL) butter, so if you can afford the calories, go for it. This is my all-time favorite cod recipe.

¹/₃ cup	flour	75 mL
1 tbsp.	curry powder	15 mL
¹/₂ tsp.	salt	2 mL
¹/₂ tsp.	pepper	2 mL
1¹/₂-2 lbs.	cod fillets (8 pieces, ³/₄-1" [2-2.5 cm] thick)	750 g-1 kg
¹/₄ cup	butter	60 mL
¹/₂ cup	slivered almonds	125 mL

Preheat oven to 250°F (180°C).

Mix the flour, curry powder, salt and pepper in a bowl. Dip the fish in the flour mixture and turn to coat several times, pressing down lightly.

Melt the butter in a large frying pan over medium-high heat. Cook the fish about 4-5 minutes per side. Put on a plate in the oven to keep hot.

Add the almonds to the frying pan. Stir and cook until the almonds are lightly browned, being careful not to burn them, about 3 minutes. Pour the almonds and pan juices over the fish and serve.

To Serve: Serve with Newfoundland Turnip Bake, page 87, and boiled parsley potatoes, or Saffron Rice, page 96, and peas.

Note: It is often difficult to buy cod, so you may need to substitute another firm fleshed white fish.

In Newfoundland, when you've played a joke on someone, instead of saying "Just kidding you", you say "Just coddin' ya, bye!"

CORNISH HENS WITH GINGER ORANGE SAUCE

**A partial make-ahead dish.
Serves 4.**

These hens come with a fresh zesty sauce.

4 x 1½ lb.	Cornish hens	4 x 750 g
2 tbsp.	butter	30 mL
2 tbsp.	minced fresh ginger	30 mL
2 tbsp.	grated orange rind	30 mL
3 tbsp.	brown sugar	45 mL
2 tsp.	flour	10 mL
⅔ cup	freshly squeezed orange juice (about 3 oranges)	150 mL
¼ cup	sherry	60 mL
1 tbsp.	lemon juice	15 mL
4 drops	Tabasco	4 drops
½ tbsp.	cornstarch dissolved in 2 tbsp. (30 mL) water (optional)	7 mL

Preheat oven to 550°F (290°C).

Place the hens, breast side down, on a rack over a pan. Put in the oven and reduce the heat to 350°F (180°C).

In a 1-quart (1 L) pot, melt the butter over medium-low heat, add the ginger, rind, sugar and flour. Cook about 3 minutes, stirring frequently. Very slowly add the orange juice, stirring constantly. Stir in the sherry, lemon juice and Tabasco. Simmer 5 minutes. Keep warm. (The sauce only can be made ahead and gently reheated.)

Baste the hens with the ginger orange sauce after 30 minutes in the oven, then turn breast side up and baste again. Bake another 30 minutes, basting several times.

If you like a thicker sauce to serve with the birds, bring sauce to a low boil after birds are cooked. Add the cornstarch/water mixture and stir well. Simmer about 3 minutes. You can omit this step and serve the sauce "as is" (I prefer the thinner version).

To Serve: Serve with plain rice and Spinach in Butter Sauce, page 81.

CORNISH HENS WITH APPLE STUFFING
Serves 4.

These little hens are very tasty — but, as with all poultry, you must stuff them at the last minute, and make sure they are completely cooked right to the center. Sherry adds zip to the apple pecan stuffing.

2 tbsp.	sherry	30 mL
2	medium apples, diced	2
¼ cup	finely chopped pecans	60 mL
1 cup	small fresh bread cubes	250 mL
½ tsp.	cinnamon	2 mL
4 x 1½ lb.	Cornish hens	4 x 750 g

Combine the sherry, apples, pecans, bread cubes and cinnamon and mix well. Cover closely and let sit at least 1 hour.

Preheat oven to 550°F (290°C).

Squeeze the stuffing lightly in your fist and stuff into the hens' cavities.

Put the birds on a rack over a pan, breast side down, and put into the hot oven. Close the oven door and reduce the heat to 350°F (180°C).

Bake for 45 minutes. Turn the birds breast side up and continue cooking for 15 minutes, until nicely browned.

To Serve: Serve with Baked Italian Rice, page 97, and Lemony Carrots, page 86.

POULET AUX PRUNEAUX

A partial make-ahead dish.
Serves 4.

You need to pucker your lips like a Frenchman to say this one. It tastes great even if you don't usually like prunes.

¼ cup	sherry	60 mL
1 tbsp.	cornstarch	5 mL
1 cup	apple juice	250 mL
½ cup	water	125 mL
12	pitted prunes, chopped	12
8	whole cloves	8
4	whole chicken breasts (8 halves)	4

Preheat oven to 500°F (260°C).

Mix the sherry, cornstarch, apple juice and water in a small pot. Add the prunes and cloves. Bring to a simmer and cook gently for 5 minutes, stirring occasionally.

Put the chicken breasts in a single layer, in an 8" (20 cm) square glass casserole. Pour the sauce over, turning the chicken to coat. (You can make this ahead to this point, cover and refrigerate, and add an extra 5-10 minutes baking time.)

Put the uncovered casserole into the oven, close the door and reduce the heat to 350°F (180°C). Cook for 30-40 minutes, until the chicken is fully cooked, basting occasionally. Remove the cloves before serving.

To Serve: *Serve with Rice with Almonds and Celery page 97, and Carrots Parmesan, page 85.*

CHICKEN ANISE

A partial make-ahead dish.
Serves 4-6.

This has a wonderfully distinctive licorice flavor.

1 tbsp.	olive oil	15 mL
2-3 lbs.	chicken pieces (skin removed if desired)	1-1.5 kg
4	garlic cloves, crushed	4
1 tsp.	anise seed	5 mL
1 tbsp.	dried basil	15 mL
12	mushrooms, quartered	12
1	green pepper, chopped	1
1	onion, chopped	1
¼ cup	water	60 mL
19 oz.	can tomatoes, chopped	540 mL
2 tbsp.	sambuca liqueur	30 mL
⅔ cup	grated Swiss cheese	150 mL

Heat the oil over medium-high heat. Add the chicken and cook about 10 minutes, until nicely browned. (You may have to do this in 2 batches if the pan is not big enough — use another 1 tbsp. (15 mL) of oil, if necessary).

Remove the chicken and set aside. Add the garlic, anise, basil, mushrooms, green pepper and onion. Add the water 1 tbsp. (15 mL) at a time, scraping the bottom of the pan as you stir. Cook, stirring frequently, about 10 minutes. Add the tomatoes, sambuca and chicken. (You can make this ahead to this point, cover and refrigerate, and reheat gently.)

Bring to a simmer and reduce the heat to medium. Cook about 30 minutes, uncovered, stirring occasionally until the chicken is done.

To Serve: Serve over pasta and top with grated Swiss cheese. You'll need to cook about 1½ lbs. (750 g) spaghetti or linguini-type pasta.

CURRIED CHICKEN WITH FRUIT

A make-ahead dish.
Serves 6.

Deliciously sweet and spicy. No need for condiments — they're already included.

1-2 tbsp.	olive oil	15-30 mL
3	garlic cloves, crushed	3
2 tbsp.	minced fresh ginger	30 mL
4	1" (2.5 cm) dried red chili peppers	4
½	red onion, thinly sliced	½
1½-2 lbs.	chicken breast (bone-in), chopped into smaller pieces	750 g-1 kg
2 cups	mixed dried fruit (apricots, prunes, raisins)	500 mL
1 tsp.	cinnamon	5 mL
1 tsp.	coriander	5 mL
1 tsp.	cumin	5 mL
3 tbsp.	tomato paste	45 mL
1¼ cups	yogurt	300 mL
1¼ cups	coconut milk	300 mL
⅓ cup	sliced blanched almonds	75 mL

Over low heat, cook the oil, garlic, ginger, chili peppers and onion for 10 minutes, stirring often. Add the chicken, fruit and spices; cook about 10 minutes, stirring occasionally. Add the tomato paste, yogurt, coconut milk and almonds. Mix well.

Cover and cook over very low heat for several hours. Stir often. It should not boil, but an occasional bubble is okay. Remove cover for last half hour of cooking. (This can be made ahead, covered and refrigerated, and reheated gently.) Remove chili peppers before serving.

To Serve: Serve over rice. Garnish with dried fruit and fresh cilantro or flat-leaf parsley.

Variation: See notes on curry on page 99. Use ½ tbsp. (7 mL) of curry powder instead of coriander and cumin, if you wish

See photograph on page 137.

CITRUS CHICKEN
Marinating time required.
Serves 4.

This sweet and tangy chicken dish looks so colorful with the sliced fruit on top.

4-6	oranges, juice of (to equal 1 cup [250 mL])	4-6
2-3	limes, juice of (to equal ⅓ cup [75 mL])	2-3
1 tsp.	cumin	5 mL
1 tsp.	coriander	5 mL
2	garlic cloves, crushed	2
3 lbs.	chicken legs and thighs	1.5 kg
1 tbsp.	olive oil	15 mL
1	orange, sliced	1
1	lime, sliced	1

In a glass casserole, combine the orange juice, lime juice, cumin, coriander and garlic and mix well. Add chicken and turn to coat. Cover and refrigerate about 6 hours, turning once.

Preheat oven to 375°F (190°C).

Drain chicken and reserve the marinade. In a large nonstick frying pan, heat the oil and cook the chicken about 3-4 minutes per side, until lightly browned. You may need to do this in 2 or 3 batches.

Put the lightly fried chicken in single layer in a 9 x 13" (23 x 33 cm) glass casserole. Pour the marinade over and turn several times to coat well, leaving skin side up. Top with the orange and lime slices and bake for about 30-40 minutes, until fully cooked and no longer pink near the bone.

To Serve: Serve with Curried Rice, page 99 and Minted Peas, page 80.

Variation: See notes on curry, page 99. Use ½ tsp. (2 mL) of cinnamon and 1 tsp. (5 mL) curry powder instead of coriander and cumin, if you wish.

HONEY MUSTARD CHICKEN

Marinating time required.
Serves 4.

Sweet and zesty.

3 lbs.	chicken pieces	1.5 kg
2/3 cup	honey	150 mL
1/3 cup	prepared mustard (regular, hot dog variety)	150 mL
2	garlic cloves, crushed	2
1/3 cup	white wine	75 mL

Fit the chicken snugly into a 9 x 13" (23 x 33 cm) glass dish in a single layer. Mix the rest of the ingredients and pour over the chicken, turning to coat. Cover and refrigerate 2 hours to overnight.

Preheat barbecue to low heat or oven to 350°F (180°C).

Drain the marinade into a small pot. Bring to a simmer and cook, uncovered, for about 10 minutes. Reduce heat to very low. Cover and keep warm for basting and dipping.

Cook the chicken pieces over low heat on the barbecue, or on a rack over a pan in the oven, for 30-40 minutes, or longer if necessary, until well done. Turn several times, and baste with the mustard sauce occasionally.

To Serve: Serve with warm mustard sauce for dipping and Light and Zesty Pasta Salad, page 72.

POULTRY

CHICKEN CREOLE
A partial make-ahead dish.
Serves 6.

If you like really hot creole, crush the dried red chili peppers before adding.

3-4 lbs.	chicken pieces (skin removed if desired)	1.5-2 kg
¼ cup	flour	60 mL
¼ tsp.	salt	1 mL
¼ tsp.	pepper	1 mL
1 tsp.	paprika	5 mL
¼ cup	olive oil	60 mL
3	garlic cloves, crushed	3
3	1" (2.5 cm) dried red chili peppers	3
1 tbsp.	dried basil	15 mL
1	large onion, thinly sliced	1
2	green peppers, in 1" (2.5 cm) pieces	2
10	large mushrooms, quartered	10
3	celery stalks, in ½" (1.3 cm) pieces	3
3	tomatoes, chopped	3
19 oz.	can tomatoes	540 mL
1	bay leaf	1
½ cup	red wine	125 mL

Put the chicken in a plastic bag with the flour, salt, pepper and paprika, and toss to coat. In a large frying pan, heat half the oil over medium-high heat, add the chicken and cook about 5 minutes per side, until lightly browned. You will probably need to do 2 batches of chicken. Remove to a 5-quart (5 L) casserole.

Preheat oven to 350°F (180°C).

In the same frying pan, heat the other half of the oil over medium heat. Add the garlic, red chili peppers, basil, onion, green pepper, mushrooms, celery and fresh tomatoes. Cook, stirring frequently, for about 10 minutes. Add to the chicken in the casserole.

Stir in the canned tomatoes, bay leaf and wine. (You can make this ahead to this point, cover and refrigerate, and reheat gently.)

Cover and bake for 1 hour. Remove cover during last 15 minutes. Remove whole chili peppers and bay leaf before serving.

To Serve: Serve over white rice.

CHICKEN CACCIATORE
A partial make-ahead dish.
Serves 4-6.

This very easy and hearty pasta, chicken dish originated as an Italian casserole prepared by hunters. Pheasant and other game birds were probably thrown into the pot and cooked over an outdoor fire.

1-2 tbsp.	olive oil	15-30 mL
2-3 lbs.	chicken pieces (skin removed if desired)	1-1.5 kg
2	garlic cloves, crushed	2
2 tsp.	dried oregano leaves	10 mL
1/2 tsp.	pepper	2 mL
1	green pepper, chopped	1
1/2	onion, chopped	1/2
1 cup	sliced mushrooms	250 mL
14 oz.	can crushed tomatoes	398 mL
5 1/2 oz.	can tomato paste	156 mL
7 oz.	can tomato sauce	213 mL
1/2 cup	red wine	125 mL
2	tomatoes, chopped	2

In a large pot or Dutch oven, heat the oil over medium heat. Add the chicken, garlic, oregano, pepper, green pepper, onion and mushrooms. Cook, stirring frequently, for about 10 minutes, until the chicken is lightly browned.

Add the remaining ingredients and stir well. (You can make this ahead to this point, cover and refrigerate, and reheat gently.)

Simmer gently, covered, stirring occasionally, for about an hour.

To Serve: Serve over spaghetti. You'll need to cook about 1 1/2 lbs. (750 g) dry pasta.

ORIENTAL CHICKEN STIR-FRY

Marinating time required.
Serves 2-4.

This will serve 2 or 3 people by itself, or more as part of a Chinese meal, for example with Hot Spiced Beef, page 153 and/or Oriental Vegetables and Vermicelli, page 104.

1 tsp.	sesame oil	5 mL
2 tbsp.	tarragon or red wine vinegar	30 mL
1 tbsp.	dark soy sauce	15 mL
3/4 cup	chicken broth	175 mL
3/4 lb.	boneless, skinless chicken, in 1/2" (1.3 cm) pieces	365 g
1	sweet red pepper, chopped	1
1	green pepper, chopped	1
2	celery stalks, chopped	2
1	small onion, chopped	1
2 tbsp.	olive oil	30 mL
3	1" (2.5 cm) dried red chili peppers (optional)	3
2 tbsp.	cornstarch	30 mL
1/2 cup	water	125 mL
1 lb.	steamed noodles, boiled 1 minute and drained	500 g
1 tbsp.	sesame seeds	15 mL

Mix the sesame oil, vinegar, soy sauce and broth in a glass bowl. Add the chicken, red and green peppers, celery and onion and mix well. Refrigerate 2 hours or overnight, stirring occasionally. Drain and reserve the marinade.

In a large frying pan or wok, heat 1 tbsp. (15 mL) oil over high heat, add chilies and drained chicken and vegetables. Stir-fry for about 3 minutes. Add the marinade and bring to a low boil. Mix the cornstarch and water and add to the pan, stirring well. Cover and simmer 2 minutes.

In another large frying pan, heat 1 tbsp. (15 mL) oil over high heat, add the noodles and stir-fry for about 2 minutes. Put the hot noodles on a platter. Cover with the chicken/vegetable mixture. Remove the red chilies if you used them. Sprinkle with sesame seeds.

Note: Try the skinny fresh noodles available in the produce section of most grocery stores. If you can't find fresh noodles, substitute another skinny noodle, cooked and drained, such as rice vermicelli.

See photograph on the front cover.

CHICKEN TERIYAKI
Marinating time required.
Serves 4-6.

This produces very tender, slightly sweet chicken.

2 tbsp.	dark soy sauce	30 mL
1 tbsp.	sherry	156 mL
2 tbsp.	brown sugar	39 mL
2	garlic cloves, crushed	2
1 tbsp.	minced ginger	15 mL
½ cup	water	125 mL
3 lbs.	small chicken pieces	1.5 kg
½ cup	water	125 mL
1 tbsp.	cornstarch	15 mL
2 tbsp.	water	30 mL

Put the soy sauce, sherry, brown sugar, garlic, ginger and ½ cup (125 mL) water in a small pot and bring to a low boil. Cook over medium heat for about 5 minutes, uncovered. Put the chicken pieces in a shallow glass dish, pour the marinade over and turn to coat. Cover and refrigerate about 4 hours or longer, turning several times.

Preheat oven to 350°F (180°C).

Drain and reserve the marinade. Put the chicken in single layer on a rack over a pan and bake for about 30-40 minutes, until chicken is completely done and no longer pink near the bone.

Meanwhile, put the reserved marinade in a small pot and add ½ cup (125 mL) water. Bring to a low boil and cook over medium-low heat for about 5 minutes. Mix the cornstarch with 2 tbsp. (30 mL) water and stir into the marinade. Simmer about 2 minutes.

To Serve: Serve with plain rice and Lemony Carrots, page 86, with the Teriyaki Sauce on the side.

CHICKEN WITH PARMESAN & ARTICHOKES

A partial make-ahead dish.
Serves 4.

Parmesan, artichokes and garlic make a deliciously moist filling for these chicken cutlets. They are perfect for an adult dinner party.

8	thin chicken cutlets, each 4-5" (10-13 cm) square, 1½-2 lbs. (750 g-1 kg) total	8
1 cup	freshly grated Parmesan cheese	250 mL
14 oz.	can artichokes, drained and chopped	398 mL
3	garlic cloves, crushed	3
2	eggs, beaten	2
⅔ cup	fine dry bread crumbs	150 mL

Preheat oven to 375°F (190°C).

Lay the cutlets flat. Mix the Parmesan, artichokes and garlic. Make 8 tight fistfuls (cylinders) and place 1 cylinder in the center of each cutlet.

Roll up the cutlets so that the filling is fully covered. Roll the cutlets gently in egg, and then in bread crumbs.

Place in a well-greased 9 x 13" (23 x 33 cm) casserole in a single layer, rolled ends down. (You can make this ahead to this point, cover and refrigerate, and add about an extra 5-10 minutes baking time.) Bake, uncovered, for 30 minutes.

To Serve: Serve with Pepper Rice, page 96, and Gingered Broccoli, page 81.

CHICKEN STEW WITH DUMPLINGS
A partial make-ahead dish.
Serves 4.

True comfort food, perfect for a cold, wet or snowy day, which makes this a Newfoundland favorite. It looks long and time-consuming, but it really is quite easy.

1 tbsp.	olive oil	15 mL
2	garlic cloves, crushed	2
1	onion, finely chopped	1
3	celery stalks, finely chopped	3
3	carrots, finely chopped	3
1/4 cup	flour	60 mL
1/2 tsp.	ground rosemary	2 mL
1/2 tsp.	salt	2 mL
1/2 tsp.	chili powder	2 mL
3 lbs.	chicken pieces	1.5 kg
1 1/2 cups	chicken broth	375 mL
1/2 cup	white wine	125 mL
2	bay leaves	2
1 cup	flour	250 mL
2 tsp.	baking powder	10 mL
1/2 tsp.	salt	2 mL
2 tbsp.	cold butter	30 mL
1	egg plus enough milk to make 1/2 cup (125 mL)	1

In a large pot or Dutch oven, heat the oil and garlic over medium-high heat; add the onion, celery and carrots; cook and stir for about 5 minutes. Remove to a large bowl.

Meanwhile, put the flour, rosemary, salt and chili powder into a large strong plastic bag. Add the chicken pieces a few at a time and shake to coat well. Cook the chicken pieces in the large pot, scraping the bottom and turning frequently, until browned, about 5 minutes. (You may need to do 2 batches.) Put the browned chicken in the bowl with the vegetables.

Very slowly add broth and wine to the pot, stirring constantly and scraping the bottom of the pot, until smooth. Add the bay leaves, chicken and vegetables. Reduce the heat to very low, cover and simmer for about 60-70 minutes. There should be only the very tiniest bubbles, if any. (You can make this ahead to this point, cover and refrigerate, and reheat gently.)

144

CHICKEN STEW WITH DUMPLINGS
Continued

To make dumplings, mix the flour, baking powder and salt. Cut in the butter until grainy; stir in the egg and milk until moistened.

Increase the heat to medium and continue to cook until broth is bubbling lightly all over the surface. Stir well. Using a large spoon, spoon the dumpling mixture quickly onto the chicken mixture, to make about 8 dumplings. Cover at once with a tight lid and cook for 10 minutes. Serve immediately with lots of bread to soak up the gravy. Remove bay leaves.

SPICY CHICKEN SAUTÉ
A make-ahead dish.
Serves 4.

Old-fashioned, home-cooked fried chicken taste, but a fraction of the fat.

2-3 lbs.	chicken pieces (skin removed if desired)	1-1.5 kg
2-3 tbsp.	flour	30-45 mL
2 tbsp.	olive oil	30 mL
½ tsp.	salt	2 mL
1 tsp.	each curry powder and chili powder	5 mL
1	large green pepper, in 1" (2.5 cm) pieces	1
15	large mushrooms, quartered	15
1	large onion, in ½" (1.3 cm) pieces	1
2 tbsp.	brown sugar	30 mL
½ cup	white wine	125 mL

In a plastic bag, toss the chicken and flour to coat lightly. In a large frying pan over medium-high heat, cook oil, salt, curry and chili powders until the mixture sizzles, about 1 minute. Add the chicken, cover and cook about 6-8 minutes per side, until lightly browned. Add the vegetables and stir well. Reduce the heat to medium-low, cover and cook about 20 minutes, until chicken is almost done. Stir in the sugar and wine. Cover and cook 10 minutes, stirring occasionally. (You can make this ahead and reheat gently.)

To Serve: Serve with Baked Creamed Potatoes, page 92, or plain rice.

SAUERBRATEN
Marinating time required.
Serves 8.

Need an idea for Octoberfest? This is it. Start marinating 2 days ahead.

4 lbs.	round or sirloin roast	2 kg
1½ cups	water	375 mL
1½ cups	red wine vinegar	375 mL
2	onions, thinly sliced	2
1	lemon, thinly sliced	1
6	cloves	6
6	peppercorns	6
4	bay leaves	4
2 tsp.	salt	10 mL
2 tbsp.	sugar	30 mL
¼ cup	flour	60 mL
3 tbsp.	oil	45 mL
¼ cup	butter	60 mL
¼ cup	flour	60 mL
2 tsp.	sugar	10 mL
8-10	gingersnaps, crushed	8-10

Put the roast in a large stainless steel pot. Combine the water, vinegar, onions, lemon, cloves, peppercorns, bay leaves, salt and 2 tbsp. (30 mL) sugar. Pour over the beef. Cover and refrigerate for about 36 hours, turning several times throughout.

Remove meat to a plate; pat dry. Sprinkle with ¼ cup (60 mL) flour and rub in lightly. Strain marinade; discard solids and save liquid.

Using the same pot as for marinating, heat the oil over medium-high heat. Add the beef and brown lightly on all sides. Add 2 cups (500 mL) reserved marinade (save the rest for later). Bring to a simmer, cover and cook, simmering gently for 2½ hours.

About 10 minutes before the 2½ hours are up, melt the butter in a small pot over medium heat. Blend in the flour and 2 tsp. (10 mL) sugar and stir 1 minute. Slowly stir in the remaining marinade and cook until thickened slightly. Add to the beef and stir well.

SAUERBRATEN
Continued.

Continue to simmer gently for another 30 minutes or so, then add the crushed gingersnaps, stirring until dissolved.

To Serve: *Serve with Hot Potato Salad, page 94, and Red Cabbage and Rutabaga, page 85.*

SCOTCH & SIRLOIN
Marinating time is required.
Serves 4.

Great twist on basic steak barbecue.

¼ cup	Scotch whisky	60 mL
2 tbsp.	oil	30 mL
2 tbsp.	Dijon mustard	30 mL
2 lbs.	sirloin, cut into 4 steaks	1 kg

Mix the Scotch, oil and mustard until well blended. Pour into a shallow glass casserole just big enough to fit the steaks snugly. Add the steaks and turn to coat. Cover and refrigerate for 4-8 hours, turning once. Remove from the refrigerator about an hour before cooking.

Preheat barbecue to high heat.

Drain off and discard the marinade. Cook the steaks on high heat on the barbecue, about 5 minutes per side, depending on how well you like your steak cooked.

To Serve: *Serve with Green Beans with Sugared Almonds, page 82, and Scalloped Potatoes and Broccoli, page 93.*

ROAST SIRLOIN WITH MUSHROOM SAUCE

A partial make-ahead dish — sauce only.
Serves 4.

Mushroom sauce is easy and can even be made earlier in the day and reheated. It goes very well with the roast beef.

2-3 lb.	sirloin roast	1-1.5 kg
¼ cup	butter	60 mL
1½ cups	sliced fresh mushrooms	375 mL
2 tbsp.	flour	30 mL
1 cup	beef broth	250 mL
½ tsp.	Worcestershire sauce	2 mL
2 tbsp.	red wine	30 mL

Preheat oven to 500°F (260°C).

Place the roast, fat side up, on a rack over a pan. Put the roast in the oven; shut the door; wait 5 minutes and reduce the heat to 350°F (180°C). Bake for 40-60 minutes, or longer, depending on how well you like your beef cooked.

Meanwhile, melt the butter in a pot over medium-high heat. Add the mushrooms and cook until soft, about 7 minutes, stirring occasionally. Reduce the heat to medium. Add the flour and stir for about a minute. Slowly add the broth, stirring constantly until smooth. Add the Worcestershire sauce and wine, and simmer about 2 minutes. (The sauce only can be made ahead to this point, covered and refrigerated, and reheated gently.)

To Serve: Pass the sauce with the sliced roast as you would a gravy. Serve with Gingered Broccoli, page 81, baked potatoes and sliced tomatoes.

BEEF STEAK & PEPPER BRANDY SAUCE

A partial make-ahead dish — sauce only.
Serves 4.

A light peppercorn sauce that's rich and satisfying, and can be made ahead and reheated. The peppercorns can be all one color, or several colors for variety.

4 x 8 oz.	fillets, or other tender boneless steak	4 x 250 g
¼ cup	butter	60 mL
½ tbsp.	peppercorns (whole or cracked)	7 mL
½ tsp.	grated pepper	2 mL
1 tbsp.	flour	15 mL
⅔ cup	beef broth	150 mL
1 tbsp.	brandy	15 mL
2 tbsp.	35% cream (whipping cream)	30 mL

Preheat the barbecue to high temperature.

Barbecue the steaks on high heat for about 5-10 minutes per side, depending on how well you like your beef cooked.

Meanwhile, in a 1-quart (1 L) pot, melt the butter over medium heat. Add the peppercorns, pepper and flour. Cook and stir for about a minute. Very slowly, stir in the broth, continuing to stir until the sauce has thickened slightly. Stir in the brandy and then the cream. Let simmer for about a minute. (The sauce only can be made ahead, covered and refrigerated, and reheated gently.)

To Serve: Spoon sauce over individual steaks or serve on the side like a gravy. Serve with Stuffed Cheddar Potatoes, page 91, and Garlicky Carrots, page 86.

See photograph on page 155.

QUICK PEPPER STEAK

Marinating time required.
Serves 4.

A very peppery steak that works well with a less expensive cut of meat.

4 x 8 oz.	boneless blade steaks (about ¾"-1" [2-2.5 cm] thick)	4 x 250 g
2 tbsp.	peanut or olive oil	30 mL
2 tbsp.	rice or cider vinegar	30 mL
2 tbsp.	brandy	30 mL
2 tbsp.	cracked black pepper	30 mL

Fit the steaks snugly into a glass dish.

Mix the oil, vinegar and brandy and pour over the steaks. Lift the meat so the marinade goes under and around. Cover and refrigerate for 5-6 hours, turning once. Drain.

Preheat the barbecue to high heat.

Sprinkle 1 tbsp. (15 mL) black pepper on each of 2 large plates. Lay the steaks on top of the pepper on 1 plate and press gently to pick up most of the pepper. Repeat this with the other side of the steaks on the other plate.

Cook on a preheated barbecue over high heat for about 5 minutes per side (or more, if necessary) for medium rare.

To Serve: Serve with Chinese Vegetable Medley, page 88.

CROSS RIB STEAK WITH LIME
Serves 4.

You could use any other inexpensive steak here, but be sure to use a fresh lime.

2 lbs.	boneless cross rib steak (about ¾-1" [2-2.5 cm] thick)	1 kg
1	lime (must be fresh!)	1
1 tsp.	cumin	5 mL
1 tsp.	coriander	5 mL

Preheat barbecue to high.

Cut the meat into 4 steaks. Halve the lime widthwise and rub the exposed lime onto the steaks, squeezing lightly as you go, so that all the meat has been rubbed with the lime and the lime has been completely squeezed of its juice. Lightly sprinkle the cumin and coriander over both sides of the meat. Let sit for 10 minutes or so.

Cook on a preheated barbecue over high heat for about 5 minutes per side, or more, if necessary, for medium rare.

To Serve: Serve with Fresh Potato Salad, page 76.

Variation: See notes on curry on page 99. Use 2 tsp. (10 mL) of curry powder instead of coriander and cumin, if you wish.

MARINATED ROUND STEAK
Marinating time is required.
Serves 4.

A great way to add flavor and tenderness to "cheap" meat (if there is such a thing as cheap meat).

2 lbs.	round steak,or other inexpensive cut (about ¾-1" [2-2.5 cm] thick)	1 kg
12 oz.	beer	341 mL
⅓ cup	Worcestershire sauce	75 mL

Cut the meat into 4 steaks. Fit them snugly into a glass dish.

Mix the beer and Worcestershire sauce and pour over the steaks. Cover and refrigerate 2-4 hours.

Preheat barbecue to high heat.

Drain off and discard the marinade. Cook the steaks on a preheated barbecue over high heat for about 5 minutes per side, or more, if necessary, for medium rare.

To Serve: Serve with baked potatoes and Sautéed Zucchini and Tomatoes, page 82.

Temperatures vary from stove to stove and from barbecue to barbecue, so you should use your own judgement when it comes to cooking temperatures and/or cooking times. (You can buy an inexpensive oven thermometer to check.) Many recipes will say to "bake for about 40 minutes" — if you have a hot oven, check for doneness a little sooner, and if you have a slow oven, be prepared to cook it a little longer, if necessary.

HOT SPICED BEEF

Marinating time required.
Serves 2-4.

Great as part of a Chinese dinner.

12 oz.	boneless beef steak	340 g
¾ cup	beef broth	175 mL
2 tsp.	hot chili paste (e.g., sambal oelek or other very hot paste)	10 mL
2 tbsp.	hoisin sauce or 1 tbsp. [15 mL] dark soy sauce and 2 tbsp. (30 mL) brown sugar	30 mL
2 tbsp.	olive oil	30 mL
3	garlic cloves, crushed	3
2 tbsp.	minced ginger	30 mL
½ cup	slivered green pepper	125 mL
½ cup	carrot matchsticks	125 mL

Sliver the beef about the thickness of popsicle sticks and about 3" (7 cm) long. This is easier to do if the meat is slightly frozen. Put in a glass dish.

Warm the broth, add the chili paste and stir to dissolve. Mix this with the beef. Cover and refrigerate 2 hours to overnight.

Strain the marinade into a small pot. Bring to a low boil. Stir in the hoisin sauce. Simmer gently about 5 minutes.

Heat the oil, garlic and ginger over high heat. Add the strained beef, green pepper and carrot matchsticks. Stir and cook about 3 minutes, until the beef is just barely cooked. Add the sauce and stir.

To Serve: Serve over white rice.

Note: This feeds 2 people by itself, but could feed more as part of a Chinese dinner, for example with Oriental Vegetables and Vermicelli, page 104, and/or Oriental Chicken Stir-Fry, page 141.

BEEF CURRY
A make-ahead dish.
Serves 6.

Don't worry if you don't have all these spices — use a little more of those you do have and a little curry powder. For Lamb Curry, substitute lamb for the beef.

2-3 tbsp.	oil	30-45 mL
1	onion, very thinly sliced	1
½	red onion, very thinly sliced	½
2	garlic cloves, crushed	2
2 tbsp.	minced fresh ginger	30 mL
8	each, cloves and cardamoms	8
1 tbsp.	cinnamon	15 mL
2 tsp.	garam masala	10 mL
1 tsp.	coriander	5 mL
2 tsp.	cumin	10 mL
4	1" (2.5 cm) dried red chili peppers, crushed first if you like a fiery curry	4
	water as needed	
2 lbs.	round steak cut in ¾" (2 cm) cubes	1 kg
28 oz.	can tomatoes	795 mL
1 cup	yogurt	250 mL
3 tbsp.	malt vinegar	45 mL
1 tbsp.	dark soy sauce	15 mL

In a large pot, put the oil, onions, garlic, ginger, cloves, cardamoms, cinnamon, garam masala, coriander, cumin and dried chilies. Cook very slowly over low heat for 20-30 minutes, stirring frequently. Stir in 2 tbsp. (30 mL) water every 5 minutes or so to create a paste.

Add the beef and cook about 10 minutes over low heat, stirring often. Add the remaining ingredients and mix well. Cook, covered, over very low heat for about 4 hours, removing cover for the last hour or so. Remove whole chili peppers before serving. (This can be made ahead, covered and refrigerated, and reheated gently.)

To Serve: Serve with plain or coconut rice, and in small bowls, any accompaniments you like, such as coconut, raisins, chopped bananas, chutneys, yogurt, etc. Let guests help themselves.

Note: Cloves and cardamoms are small so they may be difficult to remove before serving. Warn your guests about them as you are serving.

BEEF

Beef Steak and Pepper Brandy Sauce, page 149
Oriental Vegetables & Vermicelli, page 104

ENCHILADA CASSEROLE
A partial make-ahead dish.
Serves 8.

This easy "Mexican Lasagna" is medium-hot as it is; increase or decrease the jalapeños according to your own heat preference.

28 oz.	can tomatoes	796 mL
1 tbsp.	cumin	15 mL
1 tsp.	coriander	5 mL
½ tsp.	chili garlic sauce	2 mL
1 lb.	ground beef	500 g
1	onion, finely chopped	1
1	garlic clove, crushed	1
¼ cup	minced, pickled jalapeño peppers (optional)	60 mL
10	8" (20 cm) flour tortillas	10
2 cups	grated mozzarella cheese	500 mL
½ cup	grated Cheddar cheese	125 mL

Blend the tomatoes, cumin, coriander and chili garlic sauce in a blender until smooth. Spread ½ cup (125 mL) of sauce over the bottom of a 9 x 13" (23 x 33 cm) pan.

Fry ground beef, onion and garlic over medium-high heat until the meat is fully cooked, about 10 minutes, stirring occasionally. Drain off the excess fat. Stir in the jalapeño peppers.

Preheat oven to 350°F (180°C).

Lay the tortillas flat on the counter. Place about ¹⁄₁₀ of the hamburger mixture down the center of each tortilla. Sprinkle about 1½ tbsp. (22 mL) of the mozzarella cheese on top. (Use about 1 cup (250 mL) of the mozzarella for all 10 tortillas). Roll up each tortilla and lay them side by side in the pan on top of the sauce. They should fit snugly.

Spoon the rest of the sauce evenly over tortillas. Sprinkle with remaining mozzarella and then the Cheddar. (You can make this ahead to this point, cover and refrigerate. Add 10 minutes extra baking time.) Bake, uncovered, for 40 minutes. Cut into 8 squares.

To Serve: Serve with plain rice, Rice Conquisto, page 98, or refried beans. Sour cream, yogurt, salsa, guacamole, etc. make nice accompaniments.

STUFFED GREEN PEPPERS

A partial make-ahead dish.
Serves 4.

Great Oriental flavor.

4	medium, nicely rounded green peppers	4
1½ lbs.	ground beef	750 g
3	garlic cloves, crushed	3
2 tbsp.	minced fresh ginger	30 mL
2 tbsp.	dark soy sauce	30 mL

Halve the peppers lengthwise, halving the stems also and leaving them attached to the peppers. Remove the pulp and seeds. Steam the peppers until barely tender, about 15 minutes.

Preheat oven to 350°F (180°C).

Fry ground beef, garlic and ginger over medium-high heat until the meat is fully cooked, about 10 minutes, stirring occasionally. Drain off the excess fat. Stir in the soy sauce.

Spoon the meat mixture into the pepper halves.

Choose a casserole that will hold the stuffed peppers fairly snugly so they can keep each other upright if necessary. Place the peppers stuffed-side up in the dish. (You can make this ahead to this point, cover and refrigerate, and add an extra 5 minutes baking time.)

Pour hot water into the dish (not over the peppers) so that it reaches about 1" (2.5 cm) up the sides of the dish, but not to the top of the peppers. Cover and bake for about 20 minutes.

To Serve: Serve with Rice Conquisto, page 98.

APPLE MEAT LOAF

A partial make-ahead dish.
Serves 6.

This is great meatloaf, the tang of Worcestershire sauce, and the mellow sweetness of apples and maple syrup.

1½ lbs.	lean ground beef	750 g
1 cup	dry breadcrumbs	250 mL
1	onion, minced	1
1 tsp.	Worcestershire sauce	5 mL
2	eggs, lightly beaten	2
1 tbsp.	ketchup	15 mL
½ tsp.	salt	2 mL
½ tsp.	pepper	2 mL
2	apples, peeled and grated	2
¼ cup	ketchup	60 mL
¼ cup	maple syrup or pancake syrup	60 mL

Preheat oven to 325°F (160°C).

Combine everything except ¼ cup (60 mL) ketchup and the maple syrup. Mix together well, using your hands, and form into a loaf. Put the loaf into a 4 x 8" (10 x 20 cm) loaf pan.

Combine ¼ cup (60 mL) ketchup and the maple syrup and spread over the loaf. (You can make this ahead to this point, cover and refrigerate, and add an extra 10 minutes baking time.)

Bake for 1½ hours.

To Serve: Serve with Baked Creamed Potatoes, page 92 and Minted Peas, page 80.

Note: If you have leftovers, slice about ¾" (2 cm) thick, top with a piece of Cheddar cheese, and bake at 350°F (180°C) for about 15 minutes. Serve these meatloaf cheeseburgers with crusty buns and your favorite salad for an easy meal.

VEAL PARMESAN IN WINE

A partial make-ahead dish.
Serves 6-8.

Veal is expensive but in this recipe it goes such a long way that it won't break the bank.

1 1/2 lbs.	veal scallopini, very thinly sliced or pounded	750 mL
3	eggs, well-beaten	3
1 tbsp.	milk	15 mL
3/4 cup	freshly grated (very fine) Parmesan cheese	175 mL
1/2 tsp.	salt	2 mL
1/2 tsp.	pepper	2 mL
1/2 tsp.	dried oregano leaves	2 mL
3/4 cup	fine bread crumbs	175 mL
1 1/2 cups	dry white wine	375 mL
1/3 cup	butter	75 mL

Cut the veal into about 3" (7 cm) rectangles. Combine the eggs and milk in a bowl. Combine Parmesan, spices and bread crumbs in another bowl. Dip the veal pieces into the egg and then into the bread crumb mixture. Put on waxed paper in a single layer and refrigerate for at least 1 hour. (You can make this ahead to this point, cover with waxed paper and refrigerate.)

Preheat oven to 300°F (150°C).

Put the wine in a 9 x 13" (23 x 33 cm) glass casserole and put in the oven for 10 minutes. Melt about 1 tbsp. (15 mL) of the butter over medium-high heat in a large frying pan. Cook the veal in a single layer for about 1-2 minutes per side, just until brown. You will need to do several batches. As each batch is done, place it in the wine in the oven. (There will be too much for a single layer at this point).

When all the veal has been browned, cover and bake for about 30 minutes, turning once halfway through.

To Serve: Serve with Simple Side Shells, page 108 and Baked Tomatoes, page 80.

VEAL PATTIES
A partial make-ahead dish.
Serves 4.

A very easy and zesty veal dish.

1 lb.	ground veal	500 g
1 cup	freshly grated Romano cheese	250 mL
2	tomatoes, minced, shaken in colander for 15 seconds	2
½ tsp.	ground dried marjoram	2 mL
2	garlic cloves, crushed	2
1	egg, lightly beaten	1

Preheat oven to 350°F (180°C).

Combine everything in a bowl; divide into 8 balls; press and flatten the balls into muffin cups. (You can make ahead to this point, cover and refrigerate, and add 5-10 minutes baking time.)

If the muffin cups are filled to the brim, you should put a cookie sheet underneath while baking to prevent spillage into the oven. Bake for 30 minutes.

To Serve: Serve with Cheesy Herb Fettuccine With Snow Peas and Red Pepper, page 105.

STUFFED LAMB SHOULDER

A partial make-ahead dish.
Serves 6-8.

This can be a little tricky and messy to stuff and roll, depending on the particular roast. However, once you've done the stuffing, you have super company fare!

4 cups	fresh bread cubes	1 L
2	garlic cloves, crushed	2
1/3 cup	mint sauce (store-bought or see page 78)	75 mL
1/2 tsp.	pepper	2 mL
2 x 1 1/2-2 lbs.	boneless lamb shoulders	2 x 750-1 kg
2 tbsp.	flour	30 mL
2/3 cup	beef broth	150 mL
1/3 cup	red wine	75 mL

Preheat oven to 500°F (260°C).

Combine the bread cubes, garlic, mint sauce and pepper. Lay the meat out as flat as possible, making gashes to thin and flatten more, if necessary. Spread 1/2 the stuffing over the surface of each roast, up to 1" (2.5 cm) of the edges. Roll up as best you can, trying to keep all the stuffing inside the meat. Tie around twice, snugly, and lengthwise once with strong string. (You can make this ahead to this point, cover and refrigerate, and add about an extra 10 minutes baking time.)

Put the rolled meat on a rack over a pan and put in the oven. After 10 minutes, reduce heat to 350°F (180°C). Bake for another 45 minutes. Remove from the oven and let rest on top of the stove while making gravy.

Pour off most of the fat and discard, leaving about 1-2 tbsp. (15-30 mL) in the pan. Stir in the flour, scraping bottom to remove the "scrunchins". Add the broth very slowly, stirring constantly. Stir in the wine. Bring to a low boil and let simmer for 5 minutes, stirring occasionally.

Carefully slice the roasts. Serve with the gravy on the side.

To Serve: Serve with Basil and Tarragon Roasted Potatoes, page 89, and Sauteed Zucchini and Tomatoes, page 82.

Note: If you want to use 1 large roast, say 3-4 lbs. (1.5-2 kg), add 15-30 minutes to the baking time.

LAMB FRICASÉE

A partial make-ahead dish.
Serves 4.

So fragrant, it just fills your kitchen with a wonderful smell.

1 tbsp.	olive oil	15 mL
2 tbsp.	minced ginger	30 mL
4-6	garlic cloves, crushed	4-6
1 tsp.	dried oregano leaves	5 mL
2 lb.	boneless shoulder of lamb (in 1 piece)	1 kg
1	large onion, chopped	1
1	large green pepper, chopped	1
1	large sweet red pepper, chopped	1
19 oz.	can tomatoes, chopped	540 mL
1½ cups	chicken broth	375 mL
⅔ cup	finely grated feta cheese	150 mL

Preheat oven to 325°F (160°C).

Heat the oil over medium heat in a deep 4-quart (4 L) casserole, add the ginger, garlic, oregano and lamb and cook about 10 minutes, until lamb is browned lightly on all sides. Remove the lamb to a plate.

Add the onion and green and red peppers to the casserole. Cook, stirring frequently, about 10 minutes. Add the tomatoes and chicken broth and stir well.

Add the lamb, pushing the vegetables to the side so that the lamb is completely immersed in the liquid. (You can make this ahead to this point, cover and refrigerate, and add about 15 minutes to the baking time.)

Bake, covered, for about 2½ hours. Remove the lamb to a plate and slice the meat. Skim and discard any excess fat from the surface of the vegetable mixture, add the sliced meat and put the casserole back in the oven, uncovered, for about 15 minutes.

Pass with grated feta cheese to sprinkle on top.

To Serve: Serve over orzo pasta. You'll need to cook about 12 oz. (340 g) of pasta.

BARBECUED LAMB KEBABS

Marinating time required.
Serves 6.

Delicious and tender, nice Greek lemony flavor.

1½ cups	yogurt	375 mL
6	garlic cloves, crushed	6
¼ cup	lemon juice	60 mL
3 lbs.	boneless lamb shoulder in 1½" (4 cm) cubes (trim excess fat)	1.5 L
1	red onion in 1" (2.5 cm) wide wedges	1
2	green peppers in 2" (5 cm) pieces	2
1-2 tbsp.	olive oil	15-30 mL

Mix the yogurt, garlic and lemon juice. Add the lamb and mix well. Cover and refrigerate 2 hours to overnight.

Preheat barbecue to medium-high heat.

Separate the onion wedges so they are only 3-4 layers thick. Toss the pieces of onion and green pepper with the oil.

With your hands, alternate the pieces of lamb with the vegetables on metal or soaked wooden skewers. Cook over medium-high heat on the barbecue for about 20 minutes for medium, turning occasionally.

To Serve: Serve with Roast Minted Potatoes, page 88, or plain rice. Tzatziki, page 12, is also a nice accompaniment.

Variation: Using the same amounts of yogurt, garlic and lemon juice, marinate a small whole leg of lamb, 4-5 lbs. (2.-2.5 kg), overnight in the yogurt mixture in a strong plastic bag. Turn the bag a few times so the whole piece is equally marinated. Preheat oven to 500°F (260°C). Discard marinade. Put meat on a rack over a pan and put it in the oven; close the oven door; reduce heat to 350°F (180°C). Bake about 25-30 minutes per pound (500 g).

TANGY LAMB CURRY
A make-ahead dish.
Serves 6.

Very aromatic and flavorful — a complete meal with rice.

2 lb.	lamb, in 1" (2.5 cm) cubes	1 kg
1 cup	yogurt	250 mL
4	garlic cloves, crushed	4
2 tbsp.	minced ginger	30 mL
¼ cup	lime juice	60 mL
1-2 tbsp.	olive oil	15-30 mL
4	1" (2.5 cm) dried red chili peppers	4
2 tsp.	cinnamon	30 mL
1 tsp.	each cumin and coriander	5 mL
2	large onions, very thinly sliced	2
2	green peppers, finely chopped	2
2	large tomatoes, finely chopped	2
2 tbsp.	tomato paste	30 mL
1 cup	red wine	250 mL
10 oz.	pkg. frozen chopped spinach, thawed, drained	283 g
¼ cup	raisins	60 mL
½ cup	sweet flaked coconut	125 mL

Put the lamb in a glass bowl. Combine the yogurt, garlic, ginger and lime juice and mix with the lamb. Set aside.

In a 5-quart (5 L) pot, heat the oil over low heat. Add the chili peppers, cinnamon, cumin, coriander, onion, green pepper and tomatoes. Cook over very low heat, covered, stirring occasionally, for 25 minutes. If you don't want it to be too spicy, remove the dried chilies now.

Add the lamb, marinade and the rest of ingredients. Stir well. Cook, covered, over very low heat for 4-6 hours. (Bubbles barely break the surface.) Remove the cover for the last hour of cooking so the curry will get a little thicker. Remove chili peppers before serving. (This can be made ahead, covered and refrigerated, and reheated gently.)

To Serve: Serve over plain rice. Optional accompaniments include chopped banana or apple, chutneys, hot sauce, yogurt, etc.

Note: See notes on curry on page 99. Use 1 tbsp. (15 mL) curry powder and 1 tsp. (5 mL) cinnamon instead of the cinnamon, cumin and coriander.

EASY LAMB STEW

A make-ahead dish.
Serves 4.

An easy and hearty meal, this qualifies as a curry as well as a stew.

1 tbsp.	olive oil	15 mL
2	garlic cloves, crushed	2
5	slices of ginger (size of a quarter)	5
1	onion, minced	1
3	celery stalks, thinly sliced	3
12	large mushrooms, quartered	12
1 tbsp.	curry powder	15 mL
2 tbsp.	brown sugar	30 mL
1 lb.	lamb, in 1" (2.5 cm) cubes	500 g
2 tbsp.	flour	30 mL
1 cup	beef broth	250 mL
2	bay leaves	2

Put the oil, garlic, ginger, onion, celery and mushrooms in a 3-quart (3 L) pot and cook over medium heat for about 20 minutes, covered. Stir occasionally.

Add the curry powder, brown sugar and lamb and stir well. Cook for about 10 minutes. Stir in the flour for about 1 minute. Slowly add the broth, stirring constantly. Add the bay leaves. Reduce the heat to low, cover and simmer gently for about 1 hour, stirring occasionally. Remove slices of ginger and bay leaves before serving. (This can be made ahead, covered and refrigerated, and reheated gently.)

To Serve: Serve over rice or couscous, or with egg noodles (cook about ¾-1 lb. [365-500 g] pasta).

For a one-pot supper, try using an electric wok instead of a pot. This adds a touch of flair and turns the ordinary into something just a little special.

HONEY BARBECUE SAUCE

A make-ahead sauce.
Makes about 3 cups (750 mL), enough for
6-8 lbs. (2.5-3.5 kg) of meat.

This is a sweet and spicy barbecue sauce for ribs, chicken, etc. Really slather it on thickly during the last 5 minutes of cooking.

1 tsp.	olive oil	5 mL
4	garlic cloves, crushed	4
1 tsp.	dry mustard	5 mL
1/4 cup	finely grated onion	60 mL
1/2 tsp.	cayenne	2 mL
1/2 tsp.	ground oregano	2 mL
14 oz. can	tomato sauce	398 mL
5 oz. can	tomato paste	156 mL
1/2 cup	honey	125 mL
1/3 cup	brown sugar	75 mL

Heat the oil over medium heat for about a minute; add the garlic, mustard, onion, cayenne and oregano. Cook for about 2 minutes, stirring often.

Add the tomato sauce, tomato paste, honey and brown sugar. Bring to a simmer, reduce heat to low and cook very gently for about 45 minutes, stirring occasionally.

Brush sauce over pork spareribs, chicken pieces or steaks and barbecue to your taste.

Note: This will keep, tightly covered, in the refrigerator for about 1 week.

BARBECUED SPICY RIBS
A partial make-ahead dish — sauce only. Serves 4.

Ribs with a nice zesty barbecue sauce. If you like it really hot, add an extra ½ tsp. (2 mL) Tabasco sauce.

7½ oz.	can tomato sauce	213 mL
⅓ cup	ketchup	75 mL
⅓ cup	brown sugar	75 mL
½ tsp.	Tabasco sauce	2 mL
1 tsp.	cumin	5 mL
1 tsp.	coriander	5 mL
4-5 lbs.	pork spareribs (or other type, if you prefer)	2-2.2 kg

Preheat barbecue to medium heat.

In a small pot, combine everything except the ribs. Cook over medium heat for about 10 minutes. (Sauce only can be made ahead to this point. It will keep for about a week if tightly covered and refrigerated.)

Cut the ribs to about 3 ribs per piece; brush the meat with the sauce and put it on the barbecue; reduce heat to low. Cook over low heat with the cover half closed, turning and basting frequently with sauce. Keep a close eye on the ribs so they do not burn. Cook for about 30-45 minutes, depending on the heat of your barbecue. When turning the last time, turn meaty side up and really lather on the sauce. Let sit, heat off and cover closed, for about 5 minutes.

To Serve: Serve with beans and a crunchy salad, or Pasta Vegetable Salad, page 71.

Variation: See notes on curry on page 99. Use ½ tsp. (2 mL) cinnamon, 1 garlic clove, crushed and 1 tsp. (5 mL) curry powder instead of the cumin and coriander.

NEW ORLEANS RIBS

A partial make-ahead dish.
Serves 4.

These have a wonderful sweet crunchy coating.

1 cup	cornmeal	250 mL
1 tsp.	cayenne	5 mL
1 tsp.	dry mustard	5 mL
1 tsp.	cumin	5 mL
1 tsp.	coriander	5 mL
1/2 tsp.	salt	2 mL
1/2 cup	liquid honey	125 mL
2 tbsp.	hot water	30 mL
4 lbs.	pork ribs, about 3 ribs to a piece	2 kg

Preheat oven to 400°F (200°C).

Mix the cornmeal, cayenne, mustard, cumin, coriander and salt. Spread on a plate. Mix the honey and water until smooth and brush onto the meaty side of the ribs and then press the ribs into the cornmeal mixture. Lay the ribs meaty side up in a single layer on a rack over a pan. You may need several pans. Using up any leftover honey/water, gently brush onto the ribs again, being careful not to disturb the first coating. Sprinkle some of the remaining cornmeal mixture over the top. (You can make this ahead to this point, cover and refrigerate.)

Bake for 25-35 minutes, depending on the meatiness of the ribs. Be sure the meat is fully cooked. Also, if the ribs are really meaty, lay some foil over the top after about 20 minutes to prevent the crust from burning during extended cooking.

To Serve: *Serve with Romano Potatoes, page 92, and Baked Stuffed Zucchini, page 83.*

Variation: *See notes on curry on page 99. Use 1/2 tbsp. (7 mL) of cinnamon, 1 garlic clove, crushed and 1 tsp. (5 mL) curry powder instead of the cumin and coriander.*

PORK CHOPS IN MARINADE
Marinating time required.
Serves 4.

These have an Oriental flavor, slightly sweet and salty.

2 tbsp.	oil	30 mL
1 tbsp.	dark soy sauce	15 mL
2 tbsp.	brown sugar	30 mL
2 tbsp.	Dijon mustard	30 mL
3 tbsp.	white wine	45 mL
4	large pork chops	4

Combine the oil, soy sauce, sugar, mustard and wine in a small saucepan and warm over medium heat just long enough to dissolve the sugar (or microwave to dissolve). Pour the warm marinade over the chops in a shallow glass dish and turn to coat. Refrigerate about 2-3 hours, turning once.

Preheat barbecue to medium heat.

Barbecue over medium heat for about 40 minutes, until fully cooked, adjusting the heat as necessary to keep from them burning. Turn often, basting each time with marinade.

To Serve: Serve with Pepper Rice, page 96.

PEPPERED PORK CHOPS

A partial make-ahead dish.
Serves 4.

A light crunchy coating gives these chops added texture and satisfaction.

1 cup	finely crushed cornflake crumbs	250 mL
1/2 tsp.	pepper	2 mL
1/2 tsp.	paprika	2 mL
1/4 tsp.	cayenne	1 mL
1/4 cup	milk	60 mL
1	egg, beaten	1
4	large pork chops	4

Preheat oven to 450°F (230°C).

Mix the crumbs, pepper, paprika and cayenne and spread out on a plate. Mix the milk and egg in a shallow bowl. Dip the chops in the egg/milk mixture, and then in the crumb mixture. (You can make this ahead to this point, cover and refrigerate.)

Lay the chops in a single layer on a rack over a pan. Put into the oven; shut the door and reduce heat to 375°F (190°C). Bake about 45 minutes, until the meat is completely cooked.

To Serve: Serve with Cheesy Herb Fettuccine With Snow Peas And Red Pepper, page 105.

See photograph on page 173.

BAKED BLACK BEANS & SAUSAGES

A make-ahead dish.
Serves 4.

Warm and wholesome, this is a black bean chili. Leave it to cook itself while you're skating or sledding on a wintery day — the coldest person can have the jalapeño.

1 cup	dried black beans	250 mL
¾ lb.	raw spicy sausages, in ½" (1.3 cm) pieces	375 g
1 cup	chopped celery, in ¼" (1 cm) pieces	250 mL
1 cup	chopped sweet red pepper, in ½" (1.3 cm) pieces	250 mL
1	onion, chopped	1
6	garlic cloves, skinned, whole	6
2 cups	hot chicken broth	500 mL
1 cup	hot water	250 mL
½ cup	sherry	125 mL
¼ cup	packed brown sugar	60 mL
1	jalapeño pepper, whole (optional)	1

Cover the beans with about 4 cups (1 L) boiling water, turn the heat to medium, simmer gently about 30 minutes.

Meanwhile, in a large frying pan, cook the sausages over medium heat, about 8 minutes, until lightly browned. Remove to a 3-quart (3 L) casserole. Drain off excess fat.

Preheat oven to 275°F (140°C).

In the same frying pan, cook the celery, red pepper, onion and garlic about 5 minutes, stirring frequently. Remove the vegetables to the casserole with the sausages.

Add the broth, water, sherry and brown sugar to the vegetables. Mix well. Drain the beans and stir them into the casserole. The beans should be surrounded by liquid; if not, add more water. Put the jalapeño in the center.

Cover and bake for about 6 hours or longer, until the beans are tender. Remove the cover for the last hour of cooking. (You can make this ahead, cover and refrigerate, and reheat gently.)

To Serve: Serve with thick crusty bread and Crunchy Green Salad with Raspberry Mustard Dressing, page 65.

Note: If you need to stretch it to feed another person or 2, serve it over plain rice.

PORK

DESSERTS

&

SWEETS

CREAMY ORANGE FRUIT DIP

A make-ahead dish.
Makes about 1 cup (250 mL).

A relaxing, help-yourself dessert that goes very well on a hot summer night.

4 oz.	cream cheese, softened	115 g
3 tbsp.	Grand Marnier or other orange liqueur	45 mL
1 tbsp.	sugar	15 mL
½ cup	chopped fresh oranges or well-drained and chopped, canned mandarin sections	125 mL
	favorite fresh fruit, cleaned and cut into bite-sized pieces	

With an electric beater, beat the cream cheese, liqueur and sugar until smooth. Stir in the oranges. Pour into a small attractive bowl. Put the bowl on a plate and surround it with the pieces of fruit. Cover and refrigerate until ready to serve. This is best served close to room temperature, so remove it from the refrigerator about 1 hour before serving.

Note: Most fruit can be prepared ahead. However, if you plan to use apples, bananas or other fruit that discolors easily, you will have to prepare these at the last minute.

When preparing fruits and vegetables that oxidize quickly (go brown after peeling), toss with 2 tbsp. (30 mL) lemon juice mixed with 2 tbsp. (30 mL) water. This will hold them for an hour or more, especially if you toss them again and keep them well covered. Carrots stay fresh for a day or two with this method.

FROZEN PEANUT BUTTER BANANA PIE
A make-ahead dish.
Serves 6-8.

Treat yourself to peanut butter pie, this edition is much lighter and kinder to the body, both inside and out, than the usual restaurant version.

1 cup	graham or chocolate crumbs	250 mL
2 tbsp.	sugar	30 mL
2 tbsp.	melted butter	30 mL
1 cup	peanut butter	250 mL
1 cup	icing sugar (confectioner's sugar)	250 mL
¼ cup	milk	60 mL
1 cup	mashed banana	250 mL
2	egg whites	2
½ cup	35% cream (whipping cream)	125 mL
	whipped cream and sliced bananas, for garnish	

Preheat oven to 350°F (180°C).

Mix the crumbs, sugar and butter and press lightly into a 9" (23 cm) pie pan. Bake for 10 minutes and let cool while preparing filling.

With an electric beater, beat the peanut butter, icing sugar and milk until smooth. Add the banana and beat until smooth. Set aside.

Whip the egg whites until stiff peaks form. Set aside.

Clean the beaters and whip the cream until stiff peaks form. Set aside.

Gently fold the whipped cream and then the egg whites into the peanut butter mixture. Pour gently into the pie shell and smooth the surface with a spoon. Freeze at least 4 hours in the deep freeze. Garnish with whipped cream and sliced bananas just before serving.

Note: If you are going to use the whole pie, remove it from the freezer ½ hour before serving so it will cut more easily. If you plan to use only part of the pie, running a very sharp knife under hot water will help to cut a really frozen pie, and you will not have to let it thaw slightly first. Wrap leftovers well and return to freezer immediately.

APPLE DATE PIE

A make-ahead dish.
Serves 8.

Even if you've resisted making pastry for years, give it another try with a food processor. Hey, this is easy!

1¾ cups	cake and pastry flour	425 mL
½ cup	cold butter, cut up	125 mL
½ tsp.	salt	2 mL
1 tsp.	sugar	5 mL
3-4 tbsp.	ice water	45-60 mL
4 cups	thinly sliced apples	1 L
2 tbsp.	lemon juice	30 mL
½ cup	brown sugar	125 mL
1 tbsp.	flour	15 mL
⅔ cup	minced dates	150 mL
1	egg white, beaten	1
½ tsp.	sugar	2 mL

Put flour, butter, salt and sugar into a food processor and process until butter is in very fine crumbs, about 30 seconds to 1 minute. Continue to process while adding 3 tbsp. (45 mL) ice water. If dough still seems dry, add a little more water until it starts to pull away from the sides. Stop immediately. Gather dough together and put it into the refrigerator to chill for about 30 minutes. (Now you can slice those apples and mince those dates.)

Combine the apples and the lemon juice. Add the brown sugar, flour and dates and mix well.

Preheat oven to 450°F (230°C).

Roll out half the pastry into a very thin circle (sprinkle a little flour onto the counter to keep it from sticking), a little larger than an 8" (20 cm) or 9" (23 cm) pie pan. Use a flat metal spatula to help lift it off the counter in 1 piece. Fit the pastry into the pie pan and trim off the excess with a sharp knife.

Brush the bottom of the pie crust with egg white (helps to keep it from getting soggy).

Put the apple mixture into the pie shell and spread evenly. Don't spread filling onto the rim of the pie.

APPLE DATE PIE
Continued.

Roll out the remaining pastry into a thin circle, large enough to completely cover the surface of the pie, and put this on top of the apples. Press down around the edges with a fork to seal the top and bottom together. Brush the top with egg white and sprinkle ½ tsp. (2 mL) sugar over the top. Make about 6-8 small gashes in the center and around the sides of the top pastry to let steam escape.

Bake for 10 minutes, reduce heat to 375°F (190°C) and continue to bake for 30 minutes. Lay a sheet of tinfoil over the top about halfway through the baking process so the crust does not burn.

THANKS GAIL.

APPLE CRISP
A make-ahead dish.
Serves 6-8.

This traditional favorite is outstanding.

4	large apples, peeled, cored and sliced	4
8 oz.	cream cheese, softened	250 g
2 tbsp.	lemon juice	30 mL
2 tbsp.	sugar	30 mL
2	eggs	2
½ cup	flour	125 mL
1 cup	quick oats	250 mL
½ cup	brown sugar	125 mL
1 tsp.	cinnamon	5 mL
⅓ cup	cold butter, cut up	75 mL
	whipped cream	

Preheat oven to 350°F (180°C).

Spread the apples in a greased 8" (20 cm) pan. Mix the cream cheese, lemon juice, sugar and eggs until smooth. Pour evenly over the apples.

Mix the flour, oats, brown sugar and cinnamon. Cut the butter into the flour mixture until crumbly. Spread over the apple mixture. Bake for 40 minutes. (This can be made ahead and reheated just before serving.) Serve warm with whipped cream.

BROWN SUGAR PUDDING

A make-ahead dish.
Serves 8.

Think of cold wintery evenings in front of the fireplace, with a hot bowl of Brown Sugar Pudding. Even if you don't have a fireplace, you'll feel warm and comforted.

1½ cups	brown sugar	375 mL
2 tbsp.	butter	30 mL
1½ cups	boiling water	375 mL
1¾ cups	flour	425 mL
2 tbsp.	sugar	30 mL
½ tsp.	salt	2 mL
2 tsp.	baking powder	10 mL
¼ cup	cold butter, cut up	60 mL
1 cup	milk	250 mL
1	egg, beaten	1
1 tsp.	vanilla	5 mL

Preheat oven to 350°F (180°C).

Put the brown sugar and 2 tbsp. (30 mL) butter into a deep 8" (20 cm) square glass pan (the 2-quart [2 L] Corningware works well) and pour the boiling water over them. Stir to dissolve.

Combine the flour, sugar, salt and baking powder. Cut in the ¼ cup (60 mL) butter until finely crumbled.

Combine the milk, egg and vanilla, and add to the flour mixture. Stir until well mixed. Pour the thick, sticky batter into the brown sugar syrup in the pan.

Don't worry if it looks a little strange at this point, it will all come together as it bakes. Bake for about 35 minutes.

To Serve: Serve hot, warm or cold, spooning the sauce over individual portions. Ice cream or whipped cream are great additions.

LEMON CHEESECAKE — LIGHT & CREAMY

Serves 8.

Quite different from a traditional cheesecake, this light and fluffy dessert is deliciously lemony.

1 1/3 cups	graham wafer crumbs	325 mL
1/4 cup	sugar	60 mL
1/4 cup	butter, melted	60 mL
8 oz.	cream cheese, softened	250 g
1/2 cup	sour cream (regular or low-fat)	125 mL
1/4 cup	lemon juice (freshly squeezed)	60 mL
1 tbsp.	grated lemon peel (optional)	15 mL
1/2 cup	honey	125 mL
3	eggs, separated	3

Preheat oven to 350°F (180°C).

Mix the crumbs, sugar and butter and press lightly into a greased 10" (25 cm) springform pan.

With an electric beater, combine cream cheese, sour cream, lemon juice, lemon peel, honey and egg yolks and beat at high speed until well blended. Set aside.

In another bowl, with clean beaters, whip the egg whites until stiff. Fold into the cream cheese mixture. Gently spoon into crust and level the surface with a spoon. Bake for 45 minutes. The cake will fall as it cools. Let it cool to room temperature before carefully removing the pan sides.

When preheating is required, be sure the oven signal light goes off before putting the item to be baked into the oven

GRAND MARNIER CHEESECAKE

A make-ahead dish.
Serves 12.

A rich and creamy Grand Marnier-flavored baked cheesecake.

1 cup	graham wafer crumbs	250 mL
1 cup	chocolate wafer crumbs	250 mL
¼ cup	sugar	60 mL
¼ cup	melted butter	60 mL
2	eggs, beaten	2
2 oz.	Grand Marnier or other orange liqueur	60 mL
¼ tsp.	salt	1 mL
⅔ cup	brown sugar	150 mL
2 tbsp.	flour	30 mL
16 oz.	cream cheese, softened	500 g
2 tbsp.	grated orange rind	30 mL
1⅓ cups	sour cream (regular or low-fat)	325 mL
3 tbsp.	frozen orange juice concentrate	45 mL
2 tbsp.	sugar	30 mL
	fresh orange slices or canned mandarin orange segments and whipped cream for garnish	

Preheat oven to 350°F (180°C).

Mix graham and chocolate wafer crumbs, sugar and butter and press into 2 greased 9" (23 cm) pie pans or 1, 10" (25 cm) springform pan.

With an electric mixer, beat the eggs, Grand Marnier, salt, brown sugar, flour and cream cheese until smooth. Stir in the rind. Pour into the pie crusts or springform pan. Bake on the top oven rack for 25 minutes, pies (35 minutes, springform).

Meanwhile, mix the sour cream, orange juice concentrate and sugar. After the first layer has cooked, pour the sour cream mixture over the top and spread gently and evenly. Return to the oven and bake for 10 minutes, pies (15 minutes, springform). Turn off the oven and leave for 10 minutes, pies (20 minutes, springform).

Remove from the oven; cool to room temperature then chill slightly. Decorate with oranges and whipped cream.

CHOCOLATE MOUSSE CAKE
A make-ahead dish.
Serves 8-10.

Deep, Dark, and Decadent!

8 oz.	cream cheese	250 g
6 x 1 oz.	squares semisweet chocolate	6 x 30 g
20	large marshmallows	20
3	eggs	3
½ cup	sugar	125 mL
⅓ cup	cake flour	75 mL
½ cup	chocolate chips	125 mL

Preheat oven to 350°F (180°C).

In a 2-quart (2 L) pot, over low heat, melt the cream cheese, chocolate squares and marshmallows, stirring often until smooth, about 10 minutes.

Meanwhile, in a medium-sized bowl, whip the eggs for 1 minute, add the sugar and whip for 1 minute. Add the cake flour and whip for 1 minute. Add the melted chocolate mixture and whip for 1 minute.

Pour the batter into a lightly greased 10" (25 cm) springform pan and bake for 30 minutes. As soon as the cake comes out of the oven, sprinkle chocolate chips over in single layer. Let sit for about 5 minutes, by which time the chips will have softened. Spread the chips over the top surface with a knife. Slide a clean knife around the sides of the cake and remove the pan sides. Let cool.

RICH CHOCOLATE CAKE

A make-ahead dish.
Serves 12.

A rich, dense chocolate cake that doesn't need icing.

8 oz.	cream cheese, softened (regular or low-fat)	250 g
1 cup	sour cream (regular or low-fat)	250 mL
3	eggs	3
1 tsp.	vanilla	5 mL
1/4 cup	coffee liqueur (2 oz. [60 mL] bottle)	60 mL
4 x 1 oz.	squares semisweet chocolate, melted	4 x 30 g
2 cups	cake flour	500 mL
1 cup	sugar	250 mL
1/2 tsp.	salt	2 mL
2 tsp.	baking powder	10 mL
1 cup	chocolate chips	250 mL

Preheat oven to 350°F (180°C).

With an electric blender, blend the cream cheese, sour cream, eggs, vanilla, liqueur and melted chocolate until smooth.

In a large bowl, combine cake flour, sugar, salt and baking powder; mix well. Stir in the chocolate chips.

Pour the cheese mixture into the flour mixture and mix well. Pour into a lightly greased 10" (25 cm) tube pan and bake for about 50 minutes, until a knife comes out clean. Don't mind a little bit of melted chocolate chip, as long as there is no cake batter on the knife. Let cool and dust with icing sugar, if desired.

Variation: Omit sour cream and liqueur, and use instead 3/4 cup (175 mL) yogurt and 3/4 cup (175 mL) 35% cream.

SOUR CREAM PEACH CAKE

A make-ahead dish.
Serves 8.

A lovely combination of textures and tastes.

1⅓ cups	flour	325 mL
1 tsp.	baking powder	5 mL
½ cup	sugar	125 mL
⅓ cup	cold butter	75 mL
1	egg	1
¼ cup	sour cream	60 mL
2 x 14 oz.	cans sliced peaches, drained	2 x 398 mL
2 oz.	cream cheese, softened	55 g
⅔ cup	sour cream	150 mL
1	egg	1
½ cup	sugar	125 mL
1 tbsp.	flour	15 mL
1½ tbsp.	sugar	22 mL
1 tsp.	cinnamon	5 mL

Preheat oven to 400°F (200°C).

Mix the flour, baking powder and ½ cup (125 mL) sugar well. Add the butter and cut in until grainy in texture. Add the egg and sour cream and mix until it forms a slightly sticky dough. Knead for about 1 minute, then press into a greased 10" (25 cm) springform pan to cover the bottom and 1" (2.5 cm) up the sides of the pan.

Lay well-drained peach slices over the bottom of the crust.

Mix the cream cheese, sour cream, egg, ½ cup (125 mL) sugar and flour until smooth. Pour evenly over the peaches, covering all.

Mix 1½ tbsp. (22 mL) sugar and the cinnamon and sprinkle over top. Bake for 15 minutes. Reduce heat to 325°F (160°C) and continue baking for about 1 hour. Let set at room temperature and then chill several hours.

To Serve: Garnish with fresh or canned peach slices, whipped cream and fresh mint leaves, if desired.

See photograph on page 191.

PECAN APPLE CAKE

A make-ahead dish.
Serves 8-10.

A moist, dense cake, but not too heavy.

1²/₃ cups	flour	400 mL
1 cup	brown sugar	250 mL
2 tsp.	baking powder	10 mL
¹/₂ tsp.	salt	2 mL
1 tsp.	cinnamon	5 mL
¹/₃ cup	butter	75 mL
2	eggs, beaten	2
1 cup	yogurt	250 mL
2	large apples, cored and grated	2
¹/₄ cup	brown sugar	60 mL
¹/₂ cup	quick oats	125 mL
2 tbsp.	butter	30 mL
¹/₂ cup	chopped pecans	125 mL

Preheat oven to 350°F (180°C).

Combine the flour, 1 cup (250 mL) brown sugar, baking powder, salt and cinnamon and mix well. Cut in ¹/₃ cup (75 mL) butter until grainy in texture. Add the eggs, yogurt and apples, and stir until well blended. Pour into a 10" (25 cm) greased springform pan.

In a small bowl, combine ¹/₄ cup (60 mL) brown sugar, oats and 2 tbsp. (30 mL) butter, and crumble between palms of your hands. Mix in the pecans. Sprinkle this mixture over the batter in the pan. Bake for about 70 minutes, until a knife inserted in the center comes out clean. (This can be made ahead and reheated just before serving.)

To Serve: Serve warm with ice cream or whipped cream.

BASIC WHITE CAKE
A make-ahead dish.
Makes a 2 layer cake or alternatives.

If you can make a plain white cake, you can make all kinds of desserts. Just add frosting and/or fruit, maybe some jam or lemon curd between the layers, or use it in a trifle. Let your imagination come up with your own interesting combinations.

2 cups	cake and pastry flour	500 mL
2 tsp.	baking powder	10 mL
1/2 tsp.	salt	2 mL
2/3 cup	sugar	150 mL
1/2 cup	oil	125 mL
3	eggs	3
1/3 cup	yogurt	75 mL
1/3 cup	milk	75 mL
1 tsp.	vanilla	5 mL

Preheat oven to 350°F (180°C).

Mix the flour, baking powder, salt and sugar.

In another bowl, mix the oil, eggs, yogurt, milk and vanilla, and then add to the flour mixture. Stir until well combined. Pour into 2 greased 9" (23 cm) round cake pans. Bake for about 25 minutes, until a knife inserted in the center comes out clean.

STRAWBUCA SHORTCAKE
A make-ahead dish.
Serves 10.

Strawberries and sambuca complement each other well. You could use fresh strawberries and you would not need to boil the sauce for as long.

1 cup	flour	250 mL
⅔ cup	icing sugar	150 mL
½ cup	butter	125 mL
¼ cup	milk	60 mL
8 oz.	cream cheese, softened	250 g
2	eggs	2
⅔ cup	icing sugar (confectioner's sugar)	150 mL
½ cup	sugar	125 mL
½ cup	water	125 mL
3 cups	whole frozen strawberries	750 mL
3 tbsp.	sambuca liqueur	45 mL
1 tbsp.	cornstarch	15 mL

Preheat oven to 350°F (180°C).

Mix the flour and ⅔ cup (150 mL) icing sugar. Cut in the butter until grainy, then add the milk to form a sticky dough. Press and spread into lightly greased 9 x 13" (23 x 33 cm) pan, keeping as level as possible. Bake for 12 minutes.

Meanwhile, beat cream cheese, eggs and ⅔ cup (150 mL) icing sugar. When the first layer has baked for 12 minutes, remove from the oven. Pour the cream cheese layer evenly over, and return to the oven for 12 minutes.

Meanwhile, put the sugar and water into a pot and bring to a boil. When the sugar has completely dissolved, add the strawberries, bring to a low boil and cook for about 10 minutes. Turn off the heat and mash lightly with a potato masher until no large pieces remain. Mix sambuca and cornstarch and stir into the strawberry mixture for about 1 minute, until mixture thickens and becomes translucent. Pour over the cream layer when it has baked. Let cool to room temperature and then refrigerate until ready to serve.

ORANGE STREUSEL CAKE

A make-ahead dish.
Serves 6-8.

Very moist with a distinctive orange flavor.

1/3 cup	butter, softened	75 mL
1/3 cup	sugar	75 mL
2	eggs	2
2	oranges, peeled, seeded, finely chopped	2
1/2 cup	orange juice	125 mL
1 2/3 cups	flour	400 mL
1 tsp.	baking powder	5 mL
1/2 tsp.	baking soda	2 mL
1/2 tsp.	salt	2 mL
1/3 cup	brown sugar, packed	75 mL
1 tbsp.	flour	15 mL
2 tbsp.	melted butter	30 mL
1 tbsp.	orange rind (optional)	15 mL

Preheat oven to 350°F (180°C).

Cream the butter and sugar; add the eggs, oranges and juice and mix well.

In another bowl, mix 1 2/3 cups (400 mL) flour, baking powder, baking soda and salt. Add it to the butter mixture and stir well until combined. Pour into a greased 8" (20 cm) square pan.

Mix brown sugar, 1 tbsp. (15 mL) flour and melted butter. Place small dabs, about 1/2 tsp. (2 mL) each, all over the top of the batter. Bake for about 35 minutes, until a knife inserted in the center comes out clean. Sprinkle the rind over the hot cake. Top with a simple glaze if desired.

To Make the Glaze: Mix 1 cup (250 mL) icing sugar with just enough milk, 1 tsp. (15 mL) at a time, to make a glaze and then drizzle over the cake.

To Serve: Serve warm, plain or with whipped cream.

PINEAPPLE YOGURT UPSIDE DOWN CAKE

A make-ahead dish.
Serves 8.

Here's a really satisfying old-fashioned dessert that's actually pretty healthy too.

1¹⁄₃ cups	cake and pastry flour	325 mL
1 tsp.	baking powder	5 mL
¹⁄₂ tsp.	salt	2 mL
¹⁄₂ cup	sugar	125 mL
¹⁄₄ cup	butter	60 mL
1	egg	1
1 cup	yogurt	250 mL
¹⁄₂ tsp.	vanilla	2 mL
¹⁄₄ cup	pineapple juice (from canned tidbits)	60 mL
19 oz.	can pineapple tidbits, drained	540 mL
2 tbsp.	brown sugar	30 mL

Preheat oven to 350°F (180°C).

Mix the flour, baking powder, salt and sugar until well combined. Cut in the butter with a pastry blender until very fine.

In another bowl, mix egg, yogurt, vanilla and pineapple juice. Add to the dry ingredients and mix well.

Mix pineapple tidbits with the brown sugar. Put in the bottom of a lightly greased 8" (20 cm) square pan. Pour the batter over the top of the pineapple. Bake for about 50 minutes, until a knife inserted in the center comes out clean. Invert the pan over a large plate, replacing any pieces of pineapple that stick to the pan.

To Serve: Serve warm, plain or with ice cream or with whipped cream.

DESSERT

Sour Cream Peach Cake, page 185
Grand Marnier Balls, page 198

CARROT CAKE WITH LEMONY ICING

A make-ahead dish.
Serves 8.

There's nothing like a good carrot cake to get your veggies. Lower-fat substitutions are given in brackets.

1½ cups	flour	375 mL
1 tsp.	baking soda	5 mL
1 tsp.	baking powder	5 mL
1 tsp.	cinnamon	5 mL
½ tsp.	salt	2 mL
1 cup	sweet coconut	250 mL
½ cup	chopped walnuts (chopped dried apricots)	125 mL
1½ cups	grated carrot	375 mL
½ cup	oil (⅔ cup [150 mL] applesauce)	125 mL
⅔ cup	brown sugar	150 mL
½ cup	white sugar	125 mL
2	eggs, beaten	2
¼ cup	apple juice (⅓ cup [75 mL] apple juice)	60 mL

Preheat oven to 350°F (180°C).

Mix the flour, baking soda, baking powder, cinnamon, salt, coconut, walnuts and grated carrot.

In another bowl, mix the oil, brown sugar, white sugar, eggs and apple juice; then add them to the dry ingredients. Stir until well combined. Pour into a greased 8" (20 cm) square pan. Bake for about 50 minutes, until a knife inserted in the center comes out clean. Remove from the pan onto a cake rack. Cool and frost with Lemony Icing, below.

LEMONY ICING

A creamy frosting with just a hint of lemon — delicious. Enough for the top of an 8" (20 cm) cake.

4 oz.	cream cheese, softened (low-fat)	125 g
1 tbsp.	lemon juice	15 mL
1½ cups	icing sugar (confectioner's sugar)	375 mL

Whip the cream cheese and lemon juice until very smooth. Slowly add the icing sugar, beating until smooth and creamy. Use as frosting for Carrot Cake or any other favorite cake.

DOUBLE CHOCOLATE CHEESECAKE

A make-ahead dish.
Makes 24-30, 2" (5 cm) squares.

These cheesecake squares are double decadence, double delicious!

1½ cups	flour	375 mL
1 cup	icing sugar	250 mL
½ tsp.	baking powder	2 mL
⅔ cup	cold butter	150 mL
4 oz.	cold cream cheese	125 g
16 oz.	cream cheese, softened	500 g
½ cup	sweetened condensed milk	125 mL
3	eggs	3
4 x 1 oz.	squares semisweet chocolate, melted	4 x 30 g
1 tsp.	vanilla	5 mL
1 cup	chocolate chips	250 mL

Preheat oven to 350°F (180°C).

Mix the flour, icing sugar and baking powder. Chop up the butter and 4 oz. (115 g) of cream cheese and cut into the flour mixture until the texture is grainy. Press into an ungreased 9 x 13" (23 x 33 cm) pan. Bake for 10 minutes.

Meanwhile, with an electric beater, beat the 16 oz. (500 g) cream cheese until smooth. Add the sweetened condensed milk, eggs, melted chocolate and vanilla. Beat until smooth and then pour over the first layer that has baked for 10 minutes. Sprinkle chocolate chips over top. Return to oven and bake for 20 minutes.

To Serve: Let cool and cut into 2" (5 cm) squares, about 24-30, or cut into larger pieces and serve with whipped cream for a special dessert.

PEACH DATE SQUARES

A make-ahead dish.
Makes 24-30 squares.

These are not too too sweet, and the addition of the peaches gives added texture and taste that enhances this traditional treat.

1 lb.	pitted dates	500 g
2 cups	water	500 mL
1 tsp.	lemon juice	5 mL
¼ cup	sugar	60 mL
1¾ cups	flour	425 mL
2 cups	quick oats	500 mL
1 tsp.	baking soda	5 mL
1 cup	brown sugar	250 mL
1 cup	cold butter	250 mL
14 oz.	can sliced peaches, drained and sliced again	398 mL

Preheat oven to 350°F (180°C).

In a 2-quart (2 L) pot, over medium-low heat, cook the dates, water, lemon juice and sugar until smooth and paste-like, about 20 minutes at a fairly low simmer. Stir occasionally.

Meanwhile, mix the flour, oats, baking soda and sugar. Add the butter and rub mixture between the palms of your hands until crumbly. Press about 3-3½ cups (750-875 mL) of this crumble mixture into the bottom of a 9 x 13" (23 x 33 cm) pan. Top with a layer of peaches. Spread the date mixture over the peaches, and spread the rest of the crumble mixture on top, pressing lightly. Bake for 35 minutes, until just lightly browned. Cut into 2" (5 cm) squares.

To Serve: These are good served warm, either plain or with ice cream, or served cold as a square with afternoon tea.

PINEAPPLE SQUARES

A make-ahead dish.
Serves 8.

These may come to be your all-time family favorite. Chill them in the freezer until they're just slightly frozen, which makes them a little less messy to cut and remove from the pan. Unlike most squares, you need a plate and fork to eat these.

10-12	graham crackers	10-12
19 oz.	can crushed pineapple, drained	540 mL
1½ cups	icing sugar (confectioner's sugar)	375 mL
½ cup	butter, softened	125 mL
2	eggs	2
⅔ cup	35% cream (whipping cream)	150 mL

Place the graham crackers in a single layer in an 8" (20 cm) square pan, trimming to fit if necessary. Spread well-drained pineapple over the crackers.

Cream together the icing sugar, butter and eggs and spoon over the pineapple.

Whip the cream until small peaks form and spread this over the sugar layer. Chill completely before serving, at least 4 hours.

If you are using whipping cream only as a dessert topping, consider whether or not you will need an ounce or two of cream, within the expiry date, for a particular recipe. You can leave a little in the carton just in case, because for a topping there is no exact amount needed.

GRAHAM AMBROSIAS

A make-ahead dish.
Makes 30.

Decadent! Only for the true-blue sweet tooth.

30	graham crackers (approx.)	30
1 cup	butter	250 mL
½ cup	white sugar	125 mL
1 tsp.	vanilla	5 mL
1 cup	finely chopped pecans	250 mL

Preheat oven to 350°F (180°C).

Arrange the crackers next to each other on a greased cookie sheet.

In a 1-quart (1 L) saucepan, bring the butter and sugar to a low boil over medium-high heat and cook for 2 minutes. Remove from the heat. Stir in the vanilla and pecans. Spoon over the crackers as evenly as possible. Bake for 8 minutes. Remove crackers to another cookie sheet to cool, spooning any excess sauce back onto the crackers. Let cool.

GRAND MARNIER BALLS

A make-ahead dish.
Makes about 90 balls.

This may seem like a lot of liqueur, but remember it makes about 90 balls. These are great at Christmas time, and they're even better if made ahead and stored in an airtight container.

6 x 1 oz.	squares semisweet chocolate	6 x 30 g
¾ cup	corn syrup	175 mL
1 cup	Grand Marnier or other orange liqueur	250 mL
1 cup	icing sugar	250 mL
2½ cups	graham wafer crumbs	625 mL
2½ cups	chocolate wafer crumbs	625 mL
2 cups	ground pecans (7 oz. [200 grams])	500 mL
1 cup	icing sugar (confectioner's sugar)	250 mL

Melt the chocolate over low heat in a large pot. Watch carefully or it may burn. Stir frequently. Add corn syrup and liqueur and stir until well blended. Remove from heat. Add 1 cup (250 mL) icing sugar, graham crumbs, chocolate crumbs and pecans. Mix well. Put in a freezer for 15 minutes to chill enough to handle more easily.

Lay a sheet of waxed paper on the counter. Roll balls about 1" (2.5 cm) in diameter, about the size of a small walnut. When all are formed, roll each in the 1 cup (250 mL) of icing sugar. Place balls in petit-four paper cups, if desired.

Variation: Roll balls first in frothy egg white and then in chocolate hail. This is very messy to do, but the results look pretty. For variety, you could also roll the balls in cocoa or chocolate wafer crumbs.

Note: If hands get too sticky when rolling the balls, scrape excess chocolate mixture off with a dinner knife and incorporate it back into the mixture in the pot.

See photograph on page 191.

ITALIAN ALMOND COOKIES

A make-ahead dish.
Makes about 48.

These lovely cookies started out as biscotti, but never quite made it. They're not too rich or too sweet — just right for afternoon tea or with cappuccino.

2 cups	flour	500 mL
1½ cups	brown sugar	375 mL
1 tsp.	baking powder	5 mL
⅓ cup	cold butter	75 mL
½ cup	grated semisweet chocolate	125 mL
1 cup	sliced blanched almonds	250 mL
½ tsp.	almond extract	2 mL
2	eggs, plus enough milk to make ¾ cup (175 mL)	2

Preheat oven to 350°F (180°C).

Mix the flour, sugar and baking powder. Cut in butter with a pastry blender until grainy. Stir in the chocolate and almonds.

Combine the extract with the eggs and milk. Stir into the flour mixture until fully combined.

Roll into about 1½" (4 cm) balls, place about 2" (5 cm) apart on a lightly greased cookie sheet and flatten slightly with a fork. Bake for about 10 minutes.

PEANUT BUTTER-CHOCO CHIP COOKIES

A make-ahead dish.
Makes about 48.

These cookies use peanut butter in place of the regular butter for added flavor. Kids love these — even big kids.

⅔ cup	peanut butter	150 mL
1 cup	brown sugar	250 mL
2	eggs	2
¼ tsp.	salt	1 mL
1 tsp.	vanilla	5 mL
1 tsp.	baking soda	5 mL
1 cup	quick oats	250 mL
1 cup	cake flour	250 mL
1 cup	chocolate chips	250 mL

Preheat oven to 375°F (190°C).

Beat the peanut butter and sugar together until smooth. Add the eggs and beat until smooth. Stir in the salt, vanilla and baking soda. Add the oats and flour and mix until well combined. Work in the chocolate chips. Shape into 1" (2.5 cm) balls; put on a lightly greased pan about 1" (2.5 cm) apart and press lightly with a fork. Bake on the center rack of the oven for about 8 minutes.

INDEX

D

DESSERTS & SWEETS

DRESSINGS & SAUCES

DRINKS

E

F

FRENCH

G

Share *CAN•AM Cooks* with a friend

Order *CAN•AM Cooks* at $20.00 per book plus $4.00 (total order) for shipping and handling.

Number of copies _____ x $20.00 = $_____

Postage and handling _____ = $ _____ 4.00

Subtotal _____ = $ _____

In Canada add 7% GST _____(Subtotal x .07) = $ _____

Total enclosed _____ = $ _____

Visa or Mastercard #_____ Expiry Date: _____
(circle one)
Signature _____

U.S. and international orders payable in U.S. funds./ Price is subject to change.

NAME: _____

STREET: _____

CITY: _____ PROV./STATE _____

COUNTRY _____ POSTAL CODE/ZIP _____

Please make cheque or money order payable to: **Can•Am Cooks**
  (**no C.O.D. orders**)   **1150 Eighth Avenue**
Please allow 2-3 weeks for delivery   **Regina, Saskatchewan**
                                          Canada   S4R 1C9
                                          OR FAX: 1-800-823-6829

Share *CAN•AM Cooks* with a friend

Order *CAN•AM Cooks* at $20.00 per book plus $4.00 (total order) for shipping and handling.

Number of copies _____ x $20.00 = $_____

Postage and handling _____ = $ _____ 4.00

Subtotal _____ = $ _____

In Canada add 7% GST _____(Subtotal x .07) = $ _____

Total enclosed _____ = $ _____

Visa or Mastercard #_____ Expiry Date: _____
(circle one)
Signature _____

U.S. and international orders payable in U.S. funds./ Price is subject to change.

NAME: _____

STREET: _____

CITY: _____ PROV./STATE _____

COUNTRY _____ POSTAL CODE/ZIP _____

Please make cheque or money order payable to: **Can•Am Cooks**
  (**no C.O.D. orders**)   **1150 Eighth Avenue**
Please allow 2-3 weeks for delivery   **Regina, Saskatchewan**
                                          Canada   S4R 1C9
                                          OR FAX: 1-800-823-6829